CHRIST & ISLAM

Reviving God's People @ Forum.

UNDERSTANDING

THE FAITH OF

THE MUSLIMS

James A. Beverley

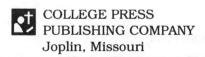

COLLEGE PRESS
PUBLISHING COMPANY
Joplin, Missouri

International Standard Book Number 0-89900-715-5

CONTENTS

This book is dedicated to
My father-in-law and mother-in-law
Norman and Phyllis Gillcash
With much love and admiration

STUDIES FOR SMALL GROUPS

Welcome to the *Studies for Small Groups* series from College Press. This series is designed for simplicity of use while giving insight into important issues of the Christian life. Some, like the present volume, will be topical studies. Others will examine a passage of Scripture for the day-to-day lessons we can learn from it.

A number of possible uses could be made of this study. Because there are a limited number of lessons, the format is ideal for new or potential Christians who can begin the study without feeling that they are tied into an overly long commitment. It could also be used for one or two months of weekly studies by a home Bible study group. The series is suitable for individual as well as group study.

Of course, any study is only as good as the effort you put into it. The group leader should study each lesson carefully before the group study session, and if possible, come up with additional Scriptures and other supporting material. Although study questions are provided for each lesson, it would also be helpful if the leader can add his or her own questions.

Neither is it necessary to complete a full lesson in one class period. If the discussion is going well, don't feel that you have to cut it off to fit time constraints, as long as the discussion is related to the topic and not off on side issues.

With *Christ & Islam*, College Press is introducing a new group of studies within the *Studies for Small Groups* series, a view of other religions of the world.

CHRIST & ISLAM

When College Press asked me to write this study guide on Islam, I was really excited. Writing this book has given me a chance to share some of the things that I have learned over many years about the way Christians should approach other religions. In this particular case, I was also delighted to share key information about Islam, the second largest world religion. I teach a course on world religions at least once a year, and so this writing has given me an opportunity to build on previous work and study related to Muhammad, the Quran, and other essentials to the Muslim's faith.

I want Christians to be encouraged by this study guide. I hope this happens in two important ways. First, my hope is that believers in Jesus will have the boldness to learn about Islam. Our witness to Muslims must be rooted in accurate knowledge that is shared in a fair and loving way. Sometimes we are scared to look at other religions. We might think that the Devil will gain an advantage or we might fear that our study will hurt our confidence in the supremacy of Christ. That leads to my second wish. This book is written with belief that Christians have nothing to fear in proclamation of the truth and beauty of the gospel of Jesus Christ. So, I encourage you and your group to read on in boldness, confident in the message that God has given in His Son.

The Christian mission to Islam today represents both peril and promise. On the negative side, there is a growing militancy in much of the Muslim world. Just as I was finishing this study guide, there were new reports of unbelievable atrocities by Muslim fanatics in Algeria and Egypt. Salman Rushdie remains in hiding because of the death threat over his infamous book *The Satanic Verses*. We must not overlook the real dangers of the militant side of Islam. Remember: there are Muslim fanatics who would target you and me for death if they believed this was necessary in their jihad or holy war.

Of course, we must not overstate the peril of Islam. Millions of Muslims deplore the random violence and terrorism adopted by Muslim militants. Our witness to the world of Islam demands that we make distinctions between different Muslim groups and beliefs. Our deep hatred for cold blooded murder done in the name of Allah must be tempered by a realization that there are Muslims who are gentle and loving. These Muslims represent the promise for a better hearing of the Gospel. Let me illustrate this latter point.

When I taught in Kenya in 1994 for African Inland Mission, my wife Gloria and I had a few days of vacation on the Kenyan coast. When we arrived in Mombassa we were nervous because we knew of reports of Muslim unrest and there were stories about thieves waiting at the train station to rob the "rich" tourists. This was unsettling for us, to say the least. We made it safely to our hotel but later we wanted to do some shopping in the city. We were worried about security.

I talked to the hotel manager and he said not to worry. He would send "Big Daddy" to take care of us for our afternoon trip. When I asked how I would recognize him, the manager replied: "Don't worry. When 'Big Daddy' comes in the lobby you will know it's him. And you will be safe in his hands." Well, we recognized Big Daddy when he arrived. This giant of a man turned out to be a devout Muslim. And we were safe in his hands.

I have often thought of him while working on this study

guide. It would be so unfair of me if I painted a picture of Islam in a way that made all Muslims out to be machine-gun-toting terrorists. I can't do this because I want to be fair to Big Daddy. He was such fun to be with, and he made us feel so secure in a land far from our home.

He knew that we were Christians and we had some interesting conversations about our beliefs. I tried my best to share the Gospel with him, but it was very hard for him to hear about Jesus without looking through the lens of Muhammad, the Quran, and his life experience as a Muslim. When we parted company with him as we took the train back to Nairobi, we hugged. I will never forget Big Daddy as long as I live.

I hope to send him a copy of this book. He reminds me of the promise represented by our shrinking global village, with air travel and modern communications. Further, there is a promising opportunity in mission simply because Muslims are coming to the west, often for reasons related to insecurity and turmoil in their own homelands. Big Daddy also reminds me that we share some common beliefs with Muslims. Thus, we can appeal to our shared view that there is one supreme Creator. But, most of all, we can point Muslims to a prophet they call Jesus, and ask them to give him very serious consideration. We long for them to see that he is more than a prophet.

This study guide is written at a popular level. I have not put in a lot of technical details about Islamic theology and philosophy, or gone into the finer points of Islamic history, or debated minor issues in the life of Muhammad or the teaching of the Quran. That would be too much for a small study guide. However, in hitting the central beliefs of Islam, I believe that I have been accurate and fair in my assessment of Islam. I invite you to join me in this journey of exploration and witness about one of the world's largest religions.

I am grateful to John Hunter and Steve Cable at College Press for their support and patience. Thanks to Keith Lee, my student research assistant, for work on bibliographical data and other help. Larry Matthews, John Wilkinson and my twin brother Bob Beverley have been a great source of encouragement, as always. As with other writing projects, I owe a lot to my wife Gloria, and to Andrea and Derek, our two children. They put up with my long hours at the computer and endured my false prophecies about when the book would be done.

James A. Beverley

Toronto, Ontario

September 1997

Preface to the Second Printing

The innocence wished for our new millennium vanished on September 11, 2001. As the World Trade Center towers collapsed and one fifth of the Pentagon disappeared, the world again faced the reality that religion can be deadly. Out of the unbelievable tragedy of that day has come a new desire among Christians to understand Islam, to sort through the different types of Muslims, and to understand Muhammad and the Quran.

I am grateful that College Press is reprinting *Christ and Islam*. I believe that my assessment of Islam remains accurate and that this guide can help Christians formulate a proper response to Muslims and their faith, even in regard to Osama bin Laden's war on America. While he reminds us of the darkest side of Islamic militancy, Christians must not equate all Muslims with him or his fellow terrorists

The message of the Gospel has taken on richer meaning since September 11. The words of Psalm 46 now have new depth: "The Lord is our refuge and strength." The promise of Jesus rings ever so much more comfortingly. "My sheep hear my voice. I know them and they follow me. I give unto them eternal life, and they shall never perish." Never perish. Never, even as buildings fall, as planes crash, as terrorists plot.

James A. Beverley
October 11, 2001

O N E

STARTING RIGHT

On almost any project, there is nothing worse than a bad start. This is ultimately true about spiritual realities. If humans head down the wrong spiritual path, all can be lost. Jesus warned in the Sermon on the Mount against those who build their lives on a bad foundation. He spoke of the multitudes who follow a way that leads to destruction. As we think together about the Christian response to Islam, what is the proper starting point?

Of course, we have to face the fact that Christians and Muslims have different starting points. The Muslim would tell you: "This matter is simple. Look to Muhammad as the final prophet. The Quran is God's Word, so follow it. This is the right starting point." Many Christians would reply: "Yes, this matter is simple. Look to Christ as the only Savior. The Bible is God's Word, so follow it. This is the right starting point."

So, starting right is not really a simple matter, from one angle. In fact, there are far more starting points than just Christian and Muslim. Think of all the different world religions and the hundreds of new religions, each with their different perspectives. Even these different groups have separate factions within them so that the starting points vary within one religion itself. Further, there are pluralists who argue that the proper route lies in recognition of the unity of all religions. Then, there are secular scholars of religion who suggest their academic path as the way to start.

This opening chapter is not about dancing with different theories about how to study religion. I have done a lot of study of these different approaches but that is a secondary issue for our purposes. We are concerned about starting right in terms of the proper Christian approach to Islam. How should "we" study religions in general and Islam in particular? What is the right start **for Christians?**

For twenty-five years I have been studying controversies about religion. I am a specialist in the study of cults, and I have also focused on the study of Christianity's relationship to world religions. Much of my Ph.D. work dealt with these two areas, and they are at the heart of my teaching work every year. I have been constantly working on developing some key ways to ensure the "right start." Let's think together about ten fundamental principles in the Christian study of Islam.

TEN KEYS IN CHRISTIAN ANALYSIS

The following keys will help us as we look at specific teachings of Islam later in this guide. Also, these principles are designed to help you in reacting to any specific religion, whether it is a new or old religion, whether it has many followers or few. While some of these keys would be shared by members of any religion or by secular scholars, others are specifically Christian in their perspective and create a unique starting point for followers of Christ.

1. *The Christian is to show* **deep and abiding concern for what is really loving.** This key is rooted in Paul's teaching in 1 Corinthians 13, obviously. A mean, bigoted faith has no place in the Christian Church. This is crucial on Islam since it is easy for us to let prejudice cloud over a loving response to the Muslim world. A loving approach means that we will

> The Christian is to show deep and abiding concern for what is really loving.

be fair and objective in our study of Islam. There may be times where real love demands strong condemnation of an aspect of Islam, but this rebuke must be set in an overall spirit of love.

2. The Christian is to show **deep care for what is really true.** *Our desire for Muslims to care about the truth must be matched by our desire for truth.* On this score, Christians have often been careless about getting facts straight about Islam. For example, it took over one thousand years for the Church to give an accurate picture of Muhammad. That's a long time to be wrong! There was a long-standing tradition of trashing Muhammad at every turn, regardless of whether the criticism was true. There is a statement from the Jewish Talmud that can help us: "Every judge who judges a judgment of truth, true to the truth of the matter, causes the glory of God to dwell in Israel."

3. Christians must **recognize the contradiction and ultimate disunity** that exists between the different religions of the world. This key is crucial in an age where Christians are told "all religions are the same." Contrary to popular opinion, the many religions of the world do not agree on even basic points. Buddhists do not believe in God. Jews and Muslims do not accept the Trinity. Mormon males believe they will develop into gods someday. Hindus believe in the worship of idols. This study guide will show the ultimate disunity of Islam and Christian faith, but this view is highly unpopular in a culture that pushes tolerance and pluralism.

4. Those who follow Jesus must also **recognize every significant agreement** between Christianity and other religions or between Christians and those of no faith. When the Quran teaches something that is true, we can celebrate our agreement. For example, the Quran teaches that Jesus is a prophet. This matches the teaching of the Bible, and so we do not need to make this a matter of debate. Muslims believe in prayer. In fact, their discipline of daily prayer can be a lesson to many Christians.

> Our desire for Muslims to care about the truth must be matched by our desire for truth.

13

The many religions of the world are not in total and complete darkness. It is not disloyal to Christ to recognize accurate claims and moral ideals in a specific religion. In medieval times Christians could hardly believe it when they discovered that Muslims were accomplished in architecture and medicine. This is no proof of the truth of Islam generally; rather, it is proof of God's common grace to all humanity.

5. Christians must **be aware of the half-truths and misleading arguments** that are used to try to bridge the gulf between Jesus and Muhammad, between the Bible and the Quran. Some Christian scholars wield the power of their intellect to defend Muhammad as a prophet or the Quran as a word from God. The case for this is very weak but is based on truth stretched to the breaking point.

For example, some Christians want to call Muhammad a prophet since he taught that there was only one God. From one angle, this was a "prophetic" word to the pagan idolatry of Saudi Arabia in Muhammad's time. However, it is inconceivable that the great title of prophet be given to a man who denied most of the essentials of the Christian faith. There is some evidence to suggest that in his later life Muhammad developed a deep hatred for Jews. Is this a prophet of God?

6. *The Christian must show **unwavering allegiance to Jesus as the only Son of God**, as God's final and ultimate Word to humanity. The Christian Church has always taught the uniqueness and supremacy of Jesus. The New Testament states clearly that Jesus is Savior and Lord over all humanity. In fact, the Islamic claim that Muhammad is the greatest is a direct contradiction to the teaching of Philippians. Paul states that because of Jesus' obedience to death on a cross, he has been given the highest name by his Father. Every knee will bow to Jesus, and every tongue will confess that he is Lord.

> The Christian must show unwavering allegiance to Jesus as the only Son of God.

7. The Christian Church must affirm that **the mercy and love of God shown in Jesus is sufficient** to answer all concerns about God's fairness in a world of religions. The Christian must resist attempts to downplay the supremacy

of Jesus or overstate the unity of religions as a means to making Christian faith more suitable to the mood of our day. The wideness of God's mercy is shown best by the grace given at Calvary. There is no love greater than the love of God shown in Jesus Christ.

Obviously, there are issues about the evangelization of Muslims that are difficult to ponder. What about Muslims who never had a chance to hear the gospel? After years of thinking on this topic, my view is that such questions must ultimately be left with God. We must avoid at all costs any human answer which suggests that there are answers more gracious than the one provided in God's grace poured out on "the old rugged cross."

> A loving Christian response does not demand any patience for evil or any toleration of atrocity.

8. Those who trust in the Christian Gospel **must not forget the wrath of God** that stands against all wickedness and evil, especially that done in the name of God. The first key in our list teaches us the importance of love. However, *a loving Christian response to Islam or any religion does not demand any patience for evil or any toleration of atrocity.* This is especially true when thinking of Islamic terrorism. The Christian must affirm the judgment of God against Muslims who kill in the name of God.

In one of my classes on Islam I had a guest who had suffered at the hands of Muslim extremists in her home country in the Middle East. It was agonizing to hear her story of capture, imprisonment, and physical and mental torture. We should take comfort here in the promise of God that he will remember the evil done to gentle lambs of Jesus who have paid an enormous price for their obedience to the gospel.

9. Christians **must be in sorrow for wickedness on the part of the church, today and throughout history.** It is easy for us to pick on Muslims for acts of terrorism in our time. However, truth and honesty demands that we acknowledge the blood in church tradition against both Muslims and Jews. One time I took a group of students to a Jewish synagogue to learn about Judaism. Rabbi Mark Dratch, a wonderful man, told us that in the larger span of history the church has brought more harm to Jewish people than Muslims, even though today it is Muslims who bring the greatest threat to Jewish people.

We must allow the gospel to critique the church. Karl Barth, one of the greatest theologians, has argued prophetically that the message of Christ must be heard by every religion including the Christian "religion." Barth's approach may have led to the popular but somewhat misleading statement that "Christianity is not a religion; it is a relationship." While Christianity *is* a world religion, it is more fundamentally about relationship with Christ. If this relationship becomes secondary, the church will engage in evil.

10. *The Christian should have a proper understanding of the* ***basics or essentials of the Christian faith.*** This will provide a framework for analysis of competing truth claims and different religious practices. Many people who have joined bizarre cult groups have simply lacked the elementary knowledge of the Bible that would have kept them from being seduced by false prophets. On Islam, any Christian who knows the Bible will not be impressed by the neglect and misunderstanding of Scripture evident in the Quran.

TESTS FOR TRUTH IN RELIGION

As we study a new or world religion or our own faith, how do we test for truth? In order to ensure comprehensive probing, Christians should apply the following multifaceted tests in approaching their own beliefs and the religion of others. These tests can be used in your individual or group study to probe the key elements of Islam. You can also use these tests to analyze the health of your church, fellowship, or denomination.

The Christian should have a proper understanding of the basics or essentials of the Christian faith.

1. The **God** Test — Does the religion recognize the one God of the Bible as the true God, the God who is the Almighty Creator of heaven and earth,

16

the God and Father of our Lord Jesus Christ, the God known as Father, Son and Holy Spirit? Do Muslims worship the same God as Christians?

Does the group in question exalt Jesus Christ as the only Eternal Savior?

2. The **Christological** Test — *Does the group in question exalt Jesus Christ as the only Eternal Savior,* as the only eternal Son of God? Does the particular religion look to Jesus as the final revelation of God? Do Muslims really have an adequate understanding of Jesus?

3. The **Biblical** Test — Do leaders in Islam really follow the Bible? Are the many and varied commands of the Bible obeyed? Are the clear and dominant teachings of Scripture believed? Does the particular religion add to, take away from, or ignore God's word?

4. The **Moral–Love** Test — Does the group in question follow the high morals of the Old and New Testament? Is love central in Islam, and is it really practiced by the leaders and members? Does Islamic faith illustrate that love is seen as the chief goal both in loving God and loving one's neighbor?

5. The **Spirituality** Test — Does the group show a desire for following the Holy Spirit? Is there a desire for purity and authentic spirituality? Are there signs of legalism and shallow ritualism that pervade the ethos of Islam?

6. The **Freedom** Test — Does Islam offer real freedom to individuals? Do Muslim leaders offer wholeness to their followers? Does the religious group abuse its members through dictatorship, secrecy, manipulation, and other forms of power-based control? Are followers mistreated sexually, or harmed financially?

7. The **Church** Test — Is Islam in continuity with the classical Christian faith? Is a specific Muslim group sectarian, rigid and narrow? Are some aspects of Islam too liberal or harmfully tolerant?

8. The **Social/Political** Test — Does Islam care for the social well-being of individuals? Do the Muslim leaders care about the political needs of humanity? Does Islam do anything

practical to address the painful realities of poverty, disease, and injustice?

9. The **Prophetic** Test — Have the leaders of the group been false prophets, either in the sense of false predictions or in the sense of careless prophetic dogmatism? Was Muhammad a false prophet?

10. The **Rational** Test — Is a given idea or practice reasonable, in keeping with wisdom and truth? Are the specific claims of Muhammad really accurate?

The complex factors noted above illustrate that *judging truth is not just an intellectual exercise.* Paul states in Ephesians that we are involved in a spiritual battle. Testing for truth demands attention to the realities of prayer, worship, and spiritual discernment. This in turn shows that our only ultimate hope for reaching truth and reaching others with that truth is grounded in the illuminating work of the Spirit.

CHRISTIAN CONFIDENCE IN THE FACE OF ISLAM

As you (and maybe a group) begin this study of Islam, a word is important about Christian confidence in reaction to the claims of Islam. I know from experience that it is unnerving to study other faiths. I remember when I first went to New York to begin my investigation of the Unification Church. I had just started teaching as a professor, was just a "rookie" in terms of studying new religions, and here I was off to New York to visit "the Moonies" (they now prefer to be called Unificationists). It was scary leaving home for this face-to-face meeting with followers of Sun Myung Moon.

Well, I did not join the Unification Church! In fact, when I was flying to New York I read quite a bit of Moon's *Divine Principle*, the Unification holy text. I saw right away that it was unbiblical in its teachings. The middle part of it was really boring, and I was not in the least convinced that Sun Myung Moon fulfills the Second Coming promised in the New Testa-

Judging truth is not just an intellectual exercise.

18

ment. By the time I got to New York, I was feeling quite secure in my Christian response to the Unification Church.

> The figure of Muhammad pales in contrast with the beauty and majesty of Jesus Christ.

Here's an example directly related to Islam. As I prepared to write the chapter on Muhammad, I was a tiny bit apprehensive. What if my detailed study of his life led me to admire him as equal to Jesus in truth and morality? Or more difficult, what if Muhammad seemed a greater spiritual leader than Jesus? I did not expect this to happen, but there was a small voice of concern in the back of my mind. What would that do to my Christian faith?

How did I handle this anxiety? Based on my trust in Christ as Savior, I felt confident that my anxiety would prove groundless. I resisted (both for your sake and mine) the easy but ultimately dishonest path of simply believing dogmatically all the nasty things I had heard about Muhammad. I chose to face the issue of his identity with integrity, and so I read careful and scholarly biographies of Muhammad. I worked hard at being objective about the details of Muhammad's life and tried my best to interpret him honestly and impartially.

In the end, I discovered that *the figure of Muhammad pales in contrast with the beauty and majesty of Jesus Christ.* Yes, I know Muslims feel differently. And, it is possible that some Christian might follow my example, read about Muhammad, and become a Muslim. All I can tell you is that my close reading of Muhammad's life relieved my concerns and reinforced my convictions that Jesus is "the way, the truth, and the life."

This does not mean that all Christians have to read the life story of every major religious leader. In fact, some Christians cannot stand the hassles connected with investigating all the theories about this or that religion. God gives each of us different gifts and callings. I view it as my task to defend the Christian faith by lengthy and comprehensive study of other religions. Then, based on such study, I can bring comfort to other believers, just as I receive comfort from them as a recipient of their gifting.

The word "courage" forms the core of encouragement. Christians need courage in understanding and witness to the Muslim world. One aim of this book is to encourage you to have confidence about the Lordship of Christ in the face of Islamic teaching and expansion. We can work together to understand Islam, assess it in light of the truth given in Jesus, and present an effective witness to Muslims that brings them the full light of the gospel.

REFLECTING ON LESSON ONE

1. What should be the major concerns of the Christian in approaching any nonbeliever for the purpose of an effective witness? *show love & concern for the person befriend them*

2. Do you agree with all ten keys in the Christian analysis of religions like Islam? Why or why not? *no, because except for the #1 God test, they are tested thru Christian beliefs. Of course, they will conflict.*

3. Is it possible to witness effectively to a person of another religion without a firm, biblical foundation of Christianity? *no, not effectively.*

4. Name the ten tests for truth in religion. What is meant by the Christological Test? the Spirituality Test? the Social/Political Test?

5. Discuss opportunities you have had to witness to people of other religions. What have you learned from these encounters? Is this an area where you believe you could be effective? *Gayle - nearly an unbeliever*

2
T W O

THE BASICS ABOUT ISLAM

There are about seven thousand books in the Library of Congress on Islam, a good number of them in Arabic. Thankfully, Islam can be understood even if we do not know Arabic or even if we have read little of the incredible collection in America's most famous library. Given the number of Muslims, the global spread of Islam, and its lengthy history, no one person can know everything about this world religion. However, the basics of Islam can be grasped quite readily.

One way to get to fundamental realities about Islam is to note its key components. First, *Islam is essentially about a very definite understanding of God.* To Muslims, Allah is the transcendent eternal Creator who is beyond comprehension. This vision of God leads to an emphasis on predestination and the total sovereignty of God. Islam is more Calvinistic in its outlook than John Calvin! In fact, some Calvinists have pointed to Islamic doctrine as proof that Calvin was correct since "even pagan Muslims see the truth about predestination."

The vision of God in Islam is of an absolute potentate, a deity who has absolute freedom in his rulings, a God who is simply above any framework of human understanding. This leads to a real sense of dependence on God but also to a lack of assurance of salvation among Muslims. There is also a pervasive fatalism and passivity in Muslim self-understanding as a consequence of the vision of God as an arbitrary being. While the Quran talks repeatedly about the mercy of Allah, this emphasis hardly influences the more dominant teaching of Allah as omnipotent Judge.

Second, Islam is essentially about **the prophet Muhammad.** While Muslims do not believe he is divine, Islamic tradition has elevated him so much that he is nearly sinless. Islam cannot be understood without knowing the dynamics of his life and the role he plays in the faith of Muslims. For centuries after Muhammad died, Muslims gathered stories about Muhammad, and these traditions (called *hadith*) have played a central role in the development of Islamic doctrine and piety.

The quickest way for Christians to see the importance of Muhammad is to realize that Jesus is viewed as inferior to him. While there is no desire in Islam to denigrate Jesus (at least in an overt or intentional way), the Christian emphasis on Jesus would be simply dismissed with a dogmatic view that the Christian tradition has missed out on the greatest human being who has ever lived: Muhammad! While Muslims hate being called Muhammadans, they do love Muhammad.

Third, Islam is essentially about **the Quran.** Jewish religion puts its emphasis on the Torah, and Christians on the New Testament. Islam places even greater stress on its holy book. Whereas both Jews and Christians have come to recognize human elements in their respective Scriptures, the vast majority of Muslims believe that the human side of the Quran is simply that it was dictated word for word to Muhammad. Most Muslims believe he was totally illiterate and consequently the Quran is a totally supernatural book.

Islam is essentially about a very definite understanding of God.

There are many Muslim religious leaders who have memorized the entire Quran. The Islamic holy book is about the same size as the New Testament. The Quran is treated with great reverence. No books are to be placed on top

22

of it. There is even consensus that it should not be translated into other languages since only the original Arabic is the very word of God. This explains why Muslims who do "translate" the Quran are quick to point out that non-Arabic renderings are nowhere equal to the Arabic version.

> In Islam there is virtually no separation of mosque and state.

Fourth, Islam is essentially about **law.** Hans Küng, the great German theologian, has stated that there are three major religious traditions that have law as a central focus: Judaism, Roman Catholicism, and Islam. Those of us who have been raised on conservative Protestant values think we have a lot of rules and regulations, but there is really no comparison between most Protestant groups and law-centered traditions like Islam.

As I did research for this study guide, I checked out various web sites on the Internet. One day I was reading Islamic laws about the duties of women in prayer. There were laws on everything from whether Muslim women could pray with nylons on (the answer is no) to whether women could pray if they had holes in their wool socks (the answer was yes as long as the holes were not too big!). This is just one example of the dominance of law in Islamic life.

Fifth, Islam is essentially about a **political and social vision.** *In Islam there is virtually no separation of mosque and state,* at least in theory. In most countries where Muslims are the majority, the political and social agenda is set by Islamic law. It is inconceivable to the Muslim mind that a religious person could possibly desire a secular state. "Why would anyone not want a nation ruled by God's principles?" the Muslim would ask.

This political and social vision of Islam must not be viewed as diverse from its spiritual vision. For Muslims they are one and the same. In many Arab countries the major political decisions are heavily influenced by the opinions of the leading Muslim teachers. In fact, Arab politicians who ignore the views of the Muslim holy men can pay for it with their lives.

The assassination of Anwar Sadat, the former Egyptian leader, was a result of the animosity he created with Muslim militants.

THE FIVE PILLARS OF ISLAM

Another way to capture the basics of Islam is to give some attention to its five pillars. This refers to five religious practices that constitute the very heart of Islamic spirituality. While Muslims around the world practice many diverse rituals (depending on their ethnic and religious background), these five pillars are common to Muslims virtually everywhere.

1. Muslims place great emphasis on quoting the *shahadah*, a one sentence statement that is the equivalent of John 3:16 for Christians. The Muslim recites this confession often: "There is no god but Allah, and Muhammad is His messenger." All that is necessary to become a Muslim is to say this with sincerity.

The *shahadah* affirms both the identity of God (Allah) and opposition to polytheism. *Implicit in the Muslim confession is disagreement with the concept of the Trinity.* The statement also affirms the centrality of Muhammad in Islam. He is not the only messenger of Allah, but he is the greatest and final prophet.

2. The Muslim is also to be a person of prayer. This is known as *salat*. The guidelines for prayer involve a command to pray towards Mecca five times daily. Also, Muslims are required to attend the prayer services every Friday at the mosque. In communal worship Muslims must wash themselves by following very specific instructions before they recite the prayers in Arabic. Even those who do not speak Arabic are expected to learn enough to be able to recite the prayers in the original.

Implicit in the Muslim confession is disagreement with the concept of the Trinity.

3. Muslims are also expected to be generous financially. This is mandated in Islam through *zakat* or alms-giving. This involves giving 2.5% of one's income to others, and this is mandatory

in some Muslim countries. The prophet Muhammad was quite generous with his wealth, and *the Quran has charity as one of its central motifs*. The practice of *zakat* is not to be confused with income tax.

> **The Quran has charity as one of its central motifs.**

4. Muslims are also told to engage in fasting. This is known in Arabic as *sawm* and involves the duty to fast during daylight hours for the month of Ramadan, which is the ninth month in the Muslim calendar. Muslims are allowed to eat and drink between sunset and sunrise. This is a special time for Muslims since they believe Ramadan was the month when Muhammad received the first revelations from Allah. The fasting ritual includes rules regarding sexual abstinence and what to do if one misses even a day of fasting during the special month.

5. Muslims are also required to make a pilgrimage to Mecca at least once in their lifetime if they can afford it. Only Muslims are allowed in their chief holy city. The pilgrimage is known as the *hajj*. The visit to Mecca usually lasts seven days and involves participation in rituals (about dress, prayer, ablution, and animal sacrifice) that date back centuries, some to the time of Muhammad. Mecca's attraction is twofold. Not only is its Muhammad's birthplace and the city to which he returned in triumph after exile in Medina, but Muslims also believe that Abraham built a temple in Mecca (called the Ka'ba) after Allah provided a ram to take the place of his son Ishmael as a sacrifice.

ISLAMIC AND CHRISTIAN DOCTRINE

Another way to capture Islamic fundamentals is to get a sense of the way Muslim doctrine compares or contrasts with Christian doctrine. We can follow the themes of Christian theology to get a sense of Islamic unity or disagreement with the classical doctrines of the Christian tradition. It should also be noted that on a few items later in this list one could find a few Muslims who might disagree with the particular view.

☆ Muslims believe in one God, as noted above, but do **not** believe in the Trinity.

☆ *Muslims believe that Jesus is a prophet of God, but **not** the Son of God.*

☆ Muslims believe the Bible is a holy book, but it has been corrupted by Jews and Christians.

☆ Muslims believe the Quran is the final revelation of God.

☆ Muslims believe Muhammad is the final prophet of God.

☆ Muslims believe God is the creator, and usually deny the theory of evolution.

☆ Muslims believe in human responsibility and do **not** believe in the Christian doctrine of original sin.

☆ Muslims believe that salvation is earned by good works, and deny the Christian view of salvation by grace alone.

☆ Muslims believe in angels and give special attention to four archangels, including Gabriel who revealed the Quran to Muhammad.

☆ Muslims believe in *jinn*, a term for created beings who seem to be different from either humans or angels.

☆ Muslims believe Satan (often called Iblis) was either an angel or jinn who rebelled against Allah.

☆ Muslims believe Allah has had five chief prophets through history who shared the same message of Islam: Noah, Abraham, Moses, Jesus, and Muhammad.

☆ Muslims believe the soul is conscious after death.

☆ Muslims believe in eternal heaven and eternal hell.

☆ Muslims believe there will be a final day of judgment when a great figure will return to crush a very evil human leader.

☆ Muslims believe those who deny the unity of God or that Muhammad is the prophet of Allah will perish.

Muslims believe that Jesus is a prophet of God, but not the Son of God.

26

JIHAD: THE SIXTH PILLAR OF ISLAM?

None of these three approaches to Islamic fundamentals bring us to a discussion of one other aspect of Islam which needs to be examined: *Jihad. Jihad is one of the most loaded words in the Muslim vocabulary.* The word has

> Jihad is one of the most loaded words in the Muslim vocabulary.

worked its way into common English usage. To most non-Muslims the word Jihad conjures up pictures of human carnage and death as Islamic militants engage in wanton acts of destruction. Jihad also brings to mind radical enforcement of Islamic law or the announcement of a death order on authors like Salman Rushdie.

☆ **Item** A beautiful Muslim girl has acid poured on her face by Muslim leaders because she allowed one wisp of hair to protrude out from under her veil.

☆ **Item** In Pakistan drinking alcohol is punishable by eighty stripes of the whip.

☆ **Item** 300,000 followers of the Baha'i faith have been persecuted in Iran.

☆ **Item** Many African Muslim leaders defend the practice of female circumcision.

☆ **Item** In Saudi Arabia squads of young men travel the streets of cities to enforce obedience to strict Islamic law.

☆ **Item** In the Sudan Christian believers from the southern part of the country are sold into slavery by Muslims.

☆ **Item** Muslim extremists blow up part of the World Trade Center in New York City.

☆ **Item** In Afghanistan females are not permitted an education according to some Muslim leaders.

What is one to make of such realities? Do they form an essential part of Islam? Some Muslims want to dismiss any hint that such acts of Jihad are relevant to orthodox Islam. Critics of Islam love to dwell on such examples as proof that Islam is a religion of the sword. I think an accurate understanding of Jihad involves a balanced assessment, one that shows that this is a complex matter.

First, *it would be unfair to dismiss all Muslims as blood-thirsty warriors in a global Islamic Jihad.* This would be like thinking that all Christians favor killings simply because some radical members of the Irish Republican Army claim to be followers of Jesus. If most Muslims were radical militants, the amount of terrorism in the world would be staggering.

Second, we must remember that Muslims often declare Jihad against one another. Thus, both Iran and Iraq declared "holy war" against each other. Millions of Muslims died as a result, but it was Muslim fighting Muslim. In most Muslim-dominated countries there are militants who have called for a Jihad against the country's political leaders because the latter fall short of following true Islam.

Third, most Muslim scholars use the term Jihad to refer to a far broader meaning of battle than a military one. It is used to indicate the war against selfishness that is at the heart of holy living. It involves the battle against temptations, and the struggle to be holy and pure, to be faithful in prayer, to obey the Quran, and to follow the model set by Muhammad himself.

Finally, we have every right to be alarmed about the actual scope of the militant side of Islam. The preceding points of balance should not dull our sense of concern about the reality of a darker side to Islamic Jihad. It will not do to simply argue that this is not pure Islam. There are Hamas suicide bombers as young as ten ready to kill on command. Many Muslims would gladly carry out the death order on Salman Rushdie. We must not be ignorant about the extremism that is at the heart of some forms of Islam.

It would be unfair to dismiss all Muslims as blood-thirsty warriors in a global Islamic Jihad.

I checked out dozens of Islamic web sites in research for this book. Most of the time the language was decent, and the tone of discussion was civil. There was nothing threatening in the religious positions that were defended, for the most part. However, there were a few exceptions, and two sites were particularly chilling, for quite different reasons. In the first case, there was language of pure hate, from a site called the Crimson Jihad.

This is the home of the Great and Holy Crimson Jihad, the Earthly hands of the Great and Holy Allah, Lord of all. If you are one of the American pig dogs who are trying to ruin Allah's beautiful world, and defame the Great and Holy Prophet of Allah, Muhammad (peace be upon him), then you are not to be welcome here. If you are one of the blasphemous Isreali [sic] pig dogs who populate our land which is not yours or belonging to you, know that you will be dying soon.

Another site championed the practice of female circumcision. What was disturbing here was the lack of empathy for the young girls who are forced to undergo such radical surgery. In reply to an American who was arguing for a ban on female circumcision, a Muslim argued for the many benefits of the practice. It was very depressing to read the zealous and illogical defense of what most humans regard as a very bizarre and inhumane ritual, one that has no blessing from the Quran or from Muhammad. The lengthy defense of female circumcision reads in part:

Here are some of the most obvious things that a girl gains when she is circumcised:

* it confers maturity and inculcates positive character traits, including the ability to endure pain and a submissive nature;

* the circumcision ritual is an enjoyable one, in which the girl is the centre of attention and receives presents and moral instruction from her elders;

* the girl will never have her conscience troubled by lustful thoughts or sensations or temptations such as masturbation.

Of course, *there are several complicating factors in understanding extreme views like this or the militant side of Islam.* Phillip Hallie has pointed out in his stimulating book *The Paradox of Cruelty* the important fact that most cruelty is done under the guise of goodness. This is true of the darkest forms of Islamic

Jihad. The leaders of Hamas who send young suicide bombers to Jewish markets in Jerusalem believe that this is the will of God. The young boys believe they will go right to paradise.

It is also true that militant Islam rises out of perceptions of real inequalities and injustices in relevant Muslim countries or in Israel. This fact does not excuse the killing and other atrocities done by Hamas or by other militant groups. However, even with total objection to Islamic Jihad, there are still hard questions to ask about democracy in Muslim countries, and social and economic equality in Israel.

Judith Miller has been a regular correspondent for *The New York Times* since 1977, and she has specialized in covering the Middle East. Her important work *God Has Ninety-Nine Names* covers the rise of militancy in ten Middle Eastern countries. It is a monumental effort of journalism, carefully weaving together historical background with contemporary events. What emerges from her reporting is the fact of a pervasive reality of militant Islam in the Middle East. She is a gifted interpreter in that she allows her readers to understand what makes militant Islam attractive to its followers without, in the least, offering any sort of blessing or excuse for its presence.

Christians could do well to emulate the model of Judith Miller. She is able to *distinguish different types of Islam so that she does not lump all Muslims together.* She is also adept at careful gathering of factual data without giving up her right to interpret the facts for herself. She is brilliant in her appreciation for everything wonderful in the Arab world, without giving up her deep appreciation for democracy and freedom.

Christians could do well to learn to distinguish different types of Islam and not lump all Muslims together.

In one place she recounts her travels in Saudi Arabia with a male friend named Abdullah. She writes: "Though I was wearing my *abayya* and a white head scarf that covered every strand of my hair, the religious police stopped us. Scowling, they ordered Abdullah to cover my face. One of them reached for

30

my head scarf to pull it down over my face. I'll never forget the hatred in his eyes. I yelled at him in English: 'Don't touch me! I am not Saudi. I am not Muslim. I am an American. American women do not wear veils.'"

> There is much glory in the story of Islam, but also a darker side, a lack of glory.

Miller is brilliant in capturing the Arab world in both its glory and shame. That duality is worth remembering about Islam in its basics. *There is much glory in the story of Islam*, since it is not simply a history of the sword, as so many critics imply. The vision of Allah has inspired so much that is noble in Islamic life. *There is also the darker side of Islam, a lack of glory.*

Of course, we have only touched on some of the basics and must learn more before we can come to a full Christian response to Islam. To that end, we will now present a fuller picture of Muhammad, the prophet of this famous and controversial religion.

31

REFLECTING ON LESSON TWO

1. Compare and contrast the Muslim and Christian view of God. How do these views affect our perception of personal power and responsibility?

2. Read Romans 3:22-30; 4:13-16; Galatians 5:1,4; Ephesians 2:8,9; 1 Timothy 1:9-11; and 2 Timothy 1:9-11. How do these verses demonstrate the difference between the Christian and Islamic perspectives on law?

3. What do you think of the Muslim idea that there is no division between political/social and religious life? Should Christians think that way? Would that work in the United States? Why or why not?

4. List the five pillars of Islam? Do we have parallels in Christianity? How are they alike or different?

5. After reading the section on *Jihad,* define this concept in one sentence. How did you respond when you heard about the bombing of the World Trade Center by Muslim terrorists?

3
T H R E E

MUHAMMAD: THE PROPHET OF GOD?

There are some religions that can be understood without reference to the founder. This is not true of Islam. Muhammad is absolutely pivotal in its origin, makeup, and ongoing life through the centuries. *The Christian response to Islam hinges on a proper assessment of this powerful figure.* If we err in a proper response to Muhammad, we will make huge blunders in understanding other aspects of Islam.

THE SIGNIFICANCE OF MUHAMMAD

Why is Muhammad so crucial in our assessment of Islam? Let me mention five significant signals of his importance. First, for Muslims Muhammad is the most important person who has ever lived. As we will examine in more detail later, Muslims place Muhammad higher than Jesus in their understanding of spiritual truth. While they do not believe that Muhammad is divine, he is to them the apex of human perfectibility. Second, Muhammad is the human agent through whom the Quran was revealed to humanity. While most Muslims would never say Muhammad wrote the Quran, he is the human recipient of what Islamic faith regards as the greatest and ultimate revelation of God.

Third, Muslims look to Muhammad as the model for proper

obedience to God. Many Muslims regard him as sinless. Muhammad's life story is examined by Muslims in order to assess what behavior should be allowed in every aspect of life. His sayings and actions became the basis of Islamic law. Stories about him circulate to this day as a source of devotional guidance. The famous Islamic theologian al-Ghazali even said that one's toenails should be cut on the basis of the example set by Muhammad.

Fourth, a negative attitude to Muhammad is deeply offensive to Muslims. The death order on Salman Rushdie is rooted in large part in his alleged contempt for the Islamic prophet expressed in the fictional work *The Satanic Verses*. Rushdie is in permanent hiding because Muslims believe he expressed malice and hatred to Muhammad. Wilfred Cantwell Smith, one of the famous scholars of Islam, believes that Muslims can tolerate an attack on Allah more than an attack on Muhammad.

Fifth, regardless of what many Christians may want, *Muhammad has had an absolutely incredible impact on history and on contemporary world realities.* Islam is the second largest religion in the world, and there are predictions that it will become the dominant religion in the next millennium. This speaks clearly of the powerful influence of Muhammad.

DIFFERENT PERSPECTIVES ON MUHAMMAD

Though we all know the crucial difference perspective makes on most topics, the impact of perspective in understanding Muhammad must be in constant focus. The Christian mission to the Muslim world demands attention to the difference that worldview and overall outlook make in the assessment of the Islamic prophet.

> Muhammad has had an absolutely incredible impact on history and on contemporary world realities.

Here's an example of the difference that perspective makes. Both in the Quran and in the traditions (*hadith*) about Muhammad there are references to physical marks on his body that are viewed as proof of his prophetic status. From the Islamic perspective, these

34

marks are simply one element in a chorus of proofs for Muhammad. What is one to make of the claim, for example, that a mole on the back of Muhammad is evidence that he is a messenger from God?

Muslims respect their scripture, their prophet, and the traditions about him.

From the perspective of a Muslim, the question is almost insulting. After all, the Quran is God's Word and it tells us that God gave this sign for his people to believe. Further, to the Muslim, how can anyone ask such a question about Muhammad? "The prophet himself would have told us if the mole was not a sign from Allah," one can hear the Muslim say.

Robert Morey, a prominent evangelical critic of Islam, minces no words in his reaction. In a pamphlet titled "By their moles ye shall know them" he expresses utter disgust that Muslims would think that a dark, hairy mole would validate Muhammad. To Morey, it is proof that Muhammad was an occult figure and that Muslims are superstitious and gullible.

The difference here is not on the basic facts about certain physical marks on Muhammad's body. The distinction is about perspective. *Muslims respect their scripture, their prophet, and the traditions about him.* Morey has no respect for any of the three. To Morey, Muslims are making a mountain out of a mole. For Muslims, Morey will suffer eternal punishment for his unbelief.

Let's consider another more serious issue. In 1993 a bomb exploded at the World Trade Center in New York City. The American people were outraged by this terrorist act and celebrated the capture of Islamic terrorists. Sheikh Abdel Rahman, a famous Egyptian Muslim, was behind the plot. Many of his followers believe that the bombing was morally defensible. Why? Because they believe that it follows the implicit teaching and explicit example of Muhammad, the great prophet of God.

For our purposes, four dominant perspectives on Muhammad in the history of interpretation are significant.

☞ The orthodox Muslim view: Muhammad is the prophet of God, the greatest human being, the moral and spiritual exemplar of humanity.

☞ The traditional Christian view: Muhammad is a tool of Satan, totally wicked, an agent of vice, an illiterate dictator, a deluded false prophet who is an enemy of the Gospel.

☞ *The current evangelical view: Muhammad fundamentally misunderstood the Gospel, is not a prophet of God, but is not as evil as the portrait presented since medieval times in the Church.*

☞ The liberal Christian view: Though Muhammad misunderstood the Gospel, he is in some sense a prophet of God who restored monotheism to a pagan culture and has brought much good to the world.

While there is some symmetry between the first and last positions, Muslims would deny the view that all religions are basically the same or that Muhammad is simply one among many messengers to God. Likewise, liberal Christians would deplore the narrow and extreme versions of Islam that have been dominant since the Quran was first written. The traditional and evangelical Christian views are unified in their fundamental objection to Muhammad, but there are obvious differences over the depth and style of complaint about the famous religious leader. Before we examine these views in further detail, our study of Islam demands knowledge of the significant moments in the life of Muhammad.

THE LIFE OF MUHAMMAD

Every founder of a world religion is subject to endless writing. There have been about 70,000 biographies of Jesus, for example. Muhammad has also been the subject of thousands of books, and there are single biographies of him that are twenty times longer than this current study guide. Despite this, the main events in Muhammad's life can be

> Muhammad fundamentally misunderstood the Gospel, is not a prophet of God, but is not totally evil.

36

grasped quite quickly and easily. Here are twenty-five key episodes in his life.

In 610 Muhammad claimed to have revelations from God.

1. Muhammad was born in Mecca about A.D. 570.

2. His father and mother both die by A.D. 576.

3. From 576 through his teen years Muhammad was cared for by his grandfather (who dies in 578) and then his uncle.

4. In 595 Muhammad (then about 25) married Khadijah, an older woman who was a merchant.

5. *In 610 Muhammad claimed to have revelations from God* in the form of mystical encounters and angelic visitations. These alleged revelations lasted till his death in 632 and are written in the Quran.

6. In 613 Muhammad began to preach his monotheistic message to the Arabs in and around Mecca. He soon received intense opposition from Arabs who believed in traditional Arabian gods.

7. In the same year Muhammad received an alleged revelation from God that stated that it was okay to worship three idols. Later, Muhammad claimed that this revelation was actually from Satan. The relevant verses were taken out of the Quran and have been called "the Satanic verses" ever since. This is the basis for the title of Salman Rushdie's infamous novel.

8. In 619 his wife passed away. Muhammad then married a woman named Sawdah. She was the first of many polygamous wives.

9. In 620 Muhammad claimed that the angel Gabriel took him (by a heavenly steed called Buruq) at night to Jerusalem where Muhammad met Moses, Abraham and Jesus. Muhammad and Gabriel ascended by ladder (called a *miraj*) through the seven heavens.

10. In 622, after seven years of opposition, Muhammad and his Muslim followers settled in Medina, 250 miles north

of Mecca. The Islamic calendar starts year one from the time of the *hijrah* or emigration to Medina.

11. In March of 623 the Muslims made their first military raid on a Meccan caravan. Muhammad chose political and military power as a strong component in his quest for spiritual dominion.

12. In April of 623 Muhammad married Aisha, who was very young, possibly just nine years old. Over time she became Muhammad's favorite wife.

13. *In February and March of 624 Muhammad commanded that prayers be made facing Mecca and that a month of fasting be instituted.*

14. On March 15, 624 the Muslims (under Muhammad's leadership) defeated their Meccan enemies at the battle of Badr. This is the most significant military victory in Muhammad's entire life and is equivalent for Muslims to the Jewish victory over Pharaoh in the Exodus.

15. A year later on March 23, 625 the Muslims barely survived the battle of Uhud. This military blow, at the hands of Meccan enemies, hurt the spiritual certainty of some of Muhammad's followers.

16. In May of 626 the chief of a Jewish clan was assassinated by Muslims, a signal of ongoing tensions between Jews and Muslims, and a warning that opposition to Muhammad came at an enormous price.

17. In 627 Muhammad married Zaynab, his cousin, who had been previously married to Zayd, Muhammad's adopted son. This marriage caused great turmoil among Muhammad's followers since he was breaking traditional Arab rules against marriage to a son's ex-wife.

In February and March of 624 Muhammad commanded that prayers be made facing Mecca.

18. In March of 627 the Meccans tried to lay siege to Medina but they lost the war.

19. In the same year Muhammad raided the Jewish clan of Qurayzah for their complicity in the prior raid on

38

Medina. Though the Jewish leaders surrendered, all the Jewish men (about 700) were beheaded and their bodies thrown into a trench. One Jewish woman was put to death, and the rest of the women (and children) were sold into slavery.

> The Ka'aba was cleansed of idols and shrines to two pagan gods were destroyed.

20. In 628 Muhammad signed a treaty with key Meccan leaders at Hudaybiyah. Though some Muslims were upset by the treaty, believing that it was not in keeping with the Islamic concept of *jihad* (or holy war), the treaty was also a signal that Meccan opposition to Muhammad had weakened in light of his growing military, political and financial resources.

21. In 629 Muhammad and 2600 followers made a pilgrimage to Mecca where they were allowed to worship at the Ka'aba or Black Stone, the site where Muslims believe Abraham and Ishmael built the first temple to God in Arabia.

22. In early January 630 Muhammad led an army of 10,000 to Mecca and conquered his enemies. *The Ka'aba was cleansed of idols and shrines to two pagan gods were destroyed.* There is a tradition that Muhammad allowed pictures of Jesus and Mary to remain on the walls.

23. On January 31, 630 Muhammad achieved military victory over Arabic tribes at the Battle of Hunayn. Later that year he led 30,000 soldiers in military raids to northern Arabia.

24. In 630 Muhammad had significant troubles dealing with jealousy and bitterness among his many wives and threatened to divorce all of them unless they lived in harmony with one another.

25. After two years of peace with Mecca, Muhammad made a final pilgrimage there in 632. He was in ill health at the time, returned to Medina, and died in the arms of Aisha, his favorite wife, on June 8, 632.

This listing of key events in Muhammad's life shows how much his life was one of political strife and military conquest. When I was doing my Ph.D. course work at the Toronto School of Theology, I had the privilege of taking a course on Christianity and other religions with Hans Küng, the famous German theologian. I can still remember Professor Küng stating: *"Jesus would not carry the sword, but Muhammad did."*

We must neither overstate or understate the reality of the sword in the life of Muhammad. He was primarily a religious leader, not a warrior, but he believed in holy war or *jihad*. He could be gentle and compassionate with his family and friends but the bloody conquests of his enemies make it impossible to call him "the prince of peace." He could be forgiving to those he conquered, but it was on his terms as the victor.

COMMON CRITICISMS OF MUHAMMAD

In understanding Muhammad one has to deal with the recurring criticisms that have dominated Western thought (both Christian and secular) and think how these measure up to what we believe is fair and true. Here are fifteen common criticisms.

1. **Claim:** Muhammad was illiterate. **Reality:** This accusation is actually borrowed from Islamic tradition where the view that Muhammad could not read or write was used positively to defend the divine authorship of the Quran. Orthodox Muslims still believe that the prophet was illiterate. Western scholars of Islam usually say that he had to have some writing skills as a merchant and political leader, though there is room for debate.

2. **Claim:** Muhammad was stupid. **Reality:** Muhammad showed extreme intelligence in many of his political, economic and military strategies. He was not trained academically, but he was far from being dumb. Though Christians have a right to believe that he was ignorant of many biblical truths, he was not stupid in the ordinary meaning of the word.

"Jesus would not carry the sword, but Muhammad did."

40

3. **Claim:** Muhammad was an idolater. **Reality:** This view is based on the Arabic background of Muhammad and the dominant pagan outlook of his culture. What is ignored here is Muhammad's radical assertion of monotheism and his contempt for idol worship.

4. **Claim:** Muhammad was simply a creature of lust and used women as sexual objects. **Reality:** The evidence suggests that Muhammad was a decent husband in many respects. However, he did have access to concubines (female slaves that provided sexual pleasure) and this runs counter to the Christian ideal. In the Islamic tradition, where Muhammad can do no wrong, there are stories that brag about Muhammad's sexual prowess.

> Muhammad allowed Christians and Jews to follow their own religion, but had no tolerance for Muslims who abandoned their faith.

5. **Claim:** Muhammad was against freedom. **Reality:** Generally speaking, this is a fair criticism. *While Muhammad allowed Christians and Jews to follow their own religion, he had no tolerance for Muslims who abandoned their faith* and was very harsh on anyone who made fun of his prophetic claims. Muhammad became more intolerant as he faced opposition and as he gained more political power.

6. **Claim:** Muhammad was a racist. **Reality:** While Muslim involvement in the slave trade (through the centuries and in our time) needs to be noted, Muhammad's first convert was a black slave. There is no indication that Muhammad was anti-Jewish on racial lines. In fact, Jews have suffered more at the hands of alleged Christians through the centuries than by the Islamic sword. Muhammad's contempt for Jews (and Christians) was rooted in his anger over religious differences, not issues of race.

7. **Claim:** Muhammad's alleged revelations were rooted in epilepsy. **Reality:** While there is some evidence that Muhammad had epileptic seizures, it is impossible to explain the Quran or his intense religious beliefs simply by reference to the fact that he may have had epilepsy.

8. **Claim:** Muhammad was anti-women. **Reality:** Muhammad was close to many women in his family life and in his religious community. He did believe that women were, in some respects, inferior to men. He had a very chauvinistic attitude about women in terms of law, religious position, and husband-wife relations. These are very divisive issues in the Islamic world today.

9. **Claim:** Muhammad had many bizarre beliefs. **Reality:** The traditions about Muhammad (*hadith*) do mention views of Muhammad that seem superstitious and bizarre. These involve wild claims about demonic power or strange beliefs about proper bathroom etiquette, for example.

10. **Claim:** Muhammad was a cold-blooded killer. **Reality:** Muhammad was the leader of an army that engaged in battle where people died. That is not what one normally means by cold-blooded killer. However, his revenge against the Jewish men of Qurayzah, and his approval of the death of some of his critics, makes it difficult to exonerate him simply by reference to the stark necessities of war.

11. **Claim:** Muhammad was a hypocrite who simply wanted power. **Reality:** While Muhammad enjoyed much power in his final years, *there is no evidence at all that he was insincere in his religious beliefs.* In fact, he illustrated his sincerity by enduring criticism and animosity from relatives and friends when he announced that he was a prophet of God. As well, he was generous with his possessions and did not live in luxury.

12. **Claim:** Muhammad believed in his faith because he hoped for a carnal heaven where sinful pleasures abound. **Reality:** There are verses in the Quran which speak of wine and women in heaven for faithful Muslim males. Later Islamic traditions amplify greatly on these themes. However, all Muslims believe that fine drink and sexual pleasure in heaven are not sinful but are the blessings of Allah. As well, Quranic verses also teach that Muslim women will enjoy the benefits of paradise.

> There is no evidence at all that Muhammad was insincere in his religious beliefs.

42

13. **Claim:** Muhammad forced people to convert to Islam by the threat of the sword. **Reality:** Muhammad never said that non-Muslims would be killed if they did not convert. The coercion that took place in his lifetime was more subtle since tribal leaders would often announce conversion to Allah, and there would be obvious pressure to follow the tribe. Also, there were times when it was financially advantageous to join with the dominant Muslim presence, and this would make conversion an attractive option.

> Islam represents the most serious opposition to Christian faith in our time.

14. **Claim:** Muhammad worshipped the moon god Allah. **Reality:** It is possible that Allah was the term sometimes used by pagan Arabs for the moon god. However, Muhammad changed the meaning of Allah by giving it reference only to the one eternal God who created everything.

15. **Claim:** Muhammad is the Anti-Christ. He hated the gospel of Jesus Christ. **Reality:** *Islam represents the most serious opposition to Christian faith in our time.* Sadly, Muhammad did not know the gospel since, as we shall see, he only had a fragmentary knowledge of the Bible. His ignorance led him to distort spiritual truth and miss many fundamental truths about Jesus.

Any summary of the life of Muhammad shows an emphasis on the sword and on military battle. While this may be somewhat consistent with certain Old Testament accounts, it is hard to reconcile Muhammad's life with the model offered by Jesus in the New Testament. In the end, the lack of symmetry between Muhammad and Jesus is the most telling objection to the suggestion that Muhammad is a prophet. As we think further on this question, we must also examine what Muhammad believed. This means a reaction to the teachings of the Quran which he believed were revealed to him directly from God.

REFLECTING ON LESSON THREE

1. Do Muslims think of Muhammad as divine? Do they put him ahead of Jesus? What is their opinion of Jesus?

2. What most upsets you about the life of Muhammad?

3. Describe the four dominant perspectives on Islam. Which would you describe as your perspective? Explain.

4. Why is it important for Christians to know the difference between truth and myth about other religions and religious leaders?

5. What are some positive characteristics of Muhammad?

4
F O U R

THE QURAN:
THE WORD OF GOD?

As great as Muhammad is to Muslims, they believe the great miracle of Islam is not its prophet, but its holy book: the Quran. It is impossible to understand Islam without coming to grips with a book regarded by a billion Muslims as the very word of God. There is a new attitude to the Quran among some Christian scholars. For centuries the Quran has been the object of ridicule by church leaders and by secular writers. In recent decades there are arguments that Christians should re-examine their negative attitude to the Islamic holy book. Hans Küng and Wilfred Cantwell Smith have both argued that the Quran should be considered, at least to some degree, as a word from God. In this chapter we will examine some key issues in a proper response to the Quran.

THE QURAN'S IMPORTANCE IN ISLAM

Muslims are the people of a book, and that book is known to English readers as the Koran or the Quran. Islamic faith holds that this book contains the very words of Allah, revealed by Gabriel to their prophet Muhammad. The Quran forms the basis for Islamic religious life, its theology, and its law. *One cannot overestimate the importance of the Quran in the shaping of the Muslim mind.* As noted earlier, there are even

45

Muslim clerics who have memorized the entire scripture, a volume about the same size as the New Testament.

It is quite easy to illustrate the powerful influence of the Quran on Muslims. When you have heard stories from Arab countries about thieves having their hands cut off for stealing, you may have thought that was unjust. According to Muslims, this is the punishment commanded by Allah. In Surah (or chapter) 5, verse 38, of the Quran we read: "As for the thief, both male and female, cut off their hands."

Christian objection to polygamy would be countered by Muslims by citation of Surah 4:3 of the Quran which allows Muslim men to have up to four wives at the same time. Islamic belief that Jesus predicted the coming of Muhammad is based on the teaching of the Quran (see 61:6 and 7:157). The view that women should be veiled is based on a single verse (24:31). The fact that the verse does not give explicit instruction on how women should be veiled explains the diverse veiling procedures in different Muslim countries.

There are two other ways to note the influence of the Quran. First, Islamic denial of key Christian beliefs is usually rooted directly in the teaching of the Quran. I remember when I first heard that Muslims do not believe that Jesus died on the cross. I thought this was to be taken as a simple declaration that they did not believe that Jesus died *for them* at Calvary. I assumed that their denial was about the *meaning* of the cross. Only later did I realize that their denial was about the *fact* of the cross.

What explains their doubt over what most people except Muslims regard as historical reality? The simple answer is that the Quran teaches that Jesus did not die on a cross. This famous teaching is given in Surah 4:157. Part of the verse reads: "they slew him not for certain." Muslims do not trust the Gospel accounts about the death of Jesus simply because this one verse has authority over all biblical material to the contrary.

One cannot overestimate the importance of the Quran in the shaping of the Muslim mind.

The importance of the Quran is also indicated by its apologetical value for Muslims. Apologetics is the term in

46

theology for defense of one's faith. The word comes from the Greek word *apologia*, a word which used to mean defense. Many Muslims claim that the Quran has advanced medical and scientific information in it, and that it contains supernatural mathematical realities.

Muslims say that the Arabic is obviously divine and that no human could write such a book. The lack of miracles in the life of Muhammad is explained by reference to the Quran as the great miracle of Islam.

THE MAJOR TEACHING OF THE QURAN

Most Christians have not read the Quran. This can be explained in several ways. First, there is simply a lack of interest in reading the holy books from other faiths. Second, some Christians would say it is dangerous to read the false teachings in Islamic scripture. Third, it is a matter of priority. "I don't read the Bible enough, so why bother with the Quran."

There is another issue to face with the Quran. Many Christians who try to read the Quran have given up simply because they find it boring and incomprehensible. Secular scholars have often been critical of the Quran's literary style and its lack of order. When I teach on world religions I usually assign reading of fifty pages in the Quran. The response is always the same: "this is boring . . . how can Muslims even think this is God's Word."

Part of the problem here is one of translation. Many English renditions of the Quran have been very poorly done. Further, it is hard for any translator to capture what is said to be the absolute beauty in the Arabic original. As well, it is not easy to enter into another religion. Reading the Quran is entering another universe of meaning for most Christians. Finally, it hurts comprehension that the Quran is not written in chronological order and that the chapters cover very diverse themes.

Despite difficulties in getting through the 114 chapters of the Quran, the main teachings of Islamic scripture are obvious, partly because they are taught over and over again throughout the book. I would suggest that there are twelve major aspects or themes in the Quran. One way for us to grasp the similarities and differences between Christianity and Islam is to explore these major themes of the Quran.

1. Allah is the one true God. There are thousands of statements about God in the Quran but its main burden is to affirm the reality of one God over against paganism (the gods and goddesses of Mecca, for example) and, to a lesser extent, a Trinitarian or Christian understanding of God. The Quran seems to imply that the Father, Son, and Mary make up the Trinity. At 5:116 it says: "O Jesus, son of Mary! Didst thou say unto mankind: Take me and my mother for two gods beside Allah?" Regardless, *Muslims have no patience for any notion of different persons in the Godhead.* In fact, the most serious sin in Islamic doctrine is known as *shirk*, which is the evil of giving God any partners.

2. Muhammad is the final prophet of God. According to the Quran, Muhammad is a gift of grace to the world (28:46-47; 72:20-23). He is inspired by God (18:110) and he is the model for moral conduct (33:21). His ministry was prophesied by both Jesus (61:6) and Moses (46:10). He is the apostle of Allah (48:29) and the seal of the prophets (33:40). If teaching about God is the first priority of the Quran, the second is affirmation of the integrity of Muhammad as the messenger of Allah.

3. The Quran is the true revelation of Allah. There are hundreds of self-referential statements in the Quran. We are told in its pages that it is an inspired message (6:19), that it is consistent (39:23), and that it is to be approached with humility (59:21). The Quran states that readers are not to entertain doubt about it (11:17).

Muslims have no patience for any notion of different persons in the Godhead.

4. Those who follow Allah and his prophet are the true believers. When you read the Quran it is clear that it is delivered in a time of great strife and pressure. It presents a picture of division between those who are "in" and

48

those who are "out." True believers are those who follow Muhammad. The rest are enemies. The increasing anxiety in the text of the Quran between believer and enemy is a clear reflection of the contours of Muhammad's life. In fact, the earlier Surahs have a more optimistic tone, before Muhammad faced the scorn and ridicule of his Meccan opponents.

> The Quran has hundreds of references to heaven or paradise but gives much more space to a doctrine of judgment and hell.

5. The joys of Heaven await the true followers of Allah. It is often said that Islam is a dreary religion and that there is no concept of joy in it. While there are aspects of Muslim life that might explain that view, the Quran spends considerable time on the promise of paradise or heaven for those who are obedient to Allah. Heaven is pictured as a garden with rivers (3:15). One section of the Quran reads: "Ye who believed our revelations and were self-surrendered, Enter the Garden, ye and your wives, to be made glad. Therein are brought round for them trays of gold and goblets, and therein is all that souls desire and eyes find sweet. And ye are immortal therein" (43:69-71).

6. Eternal Hell awaits all unbelievers. *The Quran has hundreds of references to heaven or paradise but gives much more space to a doctrine of judgment and hell.* In current Christian theology there is an attempt to moderate traditional views on hell based on re-examination of key New Testament texts. It is hard to imagine how Muslims could soften the Quranic teaching about hell since the statements are so graphic. In 4:56 Allah states: "Lo! Those who disbelieve our revelations, we shall expose them to the fire. As often as their skins are consumed we shall exchange them for fresh skins that they may taste the torment."

7. The message of the Quran has been given to Jews and Christians, the people of the Book, though they have distorted the revelations of God. Contrary to popular opinion, Muslims do not believe that their religion started with Muhammad. Rather, they believe that the Islamic faith, rooted in the eternal God, goes back to God's revelation to Adam, to Abraham and other prophets, to Jesus, and then to the greatest prophet Muhammad. The Quran gives most attention (in terms of space) to Abraham, then Moses, then Jesus, then Noah, and Joseph (Jacob's son), with brief mention given to a host of other biblical figures.

8. God has given clear signs to validate his revelations. Unbelievers are basically hypocrites who pretend to be searching for God. The revelation from God is manifest in creation (10:5-6), both in the design of nature and in humanity (56:57-59). Those who avoid God's revelation are blind, deaf, and dumb (2:17-18). The Quran is a miracle in itself and hence there is no need for Muhammad to perform miracles to authenticate his prophetic status.

9. Salvation comes to those who accept Allah's way and obey his laws. In the Quran there is a clear dividing line between believer and unbeliever, as noted above. This line is between those who obey Allah and those who do not. *Salvation is attained by human obedience to the law of God.* It is not a matter of God's unconditional grace, as in Christian doctrine. In Surah 23:102-103 the Quran states that those whose scales are heavy with good works will go to paradise, while those light in obedience will inherit hell.

10. It is imperative to join the battle on behalf of Allah and his prophet Muhammad. Though there are few commands in the Quran that could be stretched to justify modern Islamic terrorism, there are many statements about the necessity of defending Islam when it is attacked. For example, Surah 2:190 states: "Fight in the way of Allah against those who fight against you, but begin not hostilities." The Quran is a call to decision about Allah's message through Muhammad. There is a spiritual battle going on in the hearts of humanity, and this spiritual warfare sometimes justifies physical war, according to the Quran.

According to the Quran, salvation is attained by human obedience to the law of God.

11. The Quran gives guidelines on the way of righteousness and goodness. The Quran's instructions on morality

50

are not given in any particular Surahs but are scattered at random throughout the Muslim scripture. Kenneth Cragg, a leading Christian scholar of Islam, has arranged these teachings topically in his book *Readings in the Quran* (London: HarperCollins, 1988). The Quran devotes considerable space to the importance of prayer. All Muslims are to pray facing Mecca, and, if possible, every Muslim should make a pilgrimage to Mecca at least once in their life. The believer is to be a person of generosity, a notion illustrated in warnings against usury or charging interest. Believers are to be careful about sexual purity. Women in particular are to dress modestly and be very discreet in the presence of males who are not related to them.

12. Muhammad is to be followed as the model for moral and spiritual conduct. While the Quran gives general guidelines on morality, it also commends Muhammad as the ideal human to follow for goodness and purity. Surah 42 says that the prophet is a guide to the straight path. The emphasis on Muhammad led Muslims to record their memories about Muhammad (*hadith*) and these stories are often used to give moral, spiritual, and legal guidelines on topics not specifically addressed by the Quran.

A CHRISTIAN RESPONSE TO THE QURAN

Whatever else is done in a proper Christian response to the Islamic Scripture, *every Christian must take seriously the absolute importance of the Quran to the Muslim.* Some Islamic scholars suggest that the Quran is to Islam what Christ is to Christianity. We need to remember that the Quran is viewed as divine by Muslims whereas Muhammad is not. Muslims would never say that Muhammad is the incarnate Word of God. The utter supremacy of the Quran to Muslims is a reality that Christians must not forget.

Beyond this, how do we respond to the Quran? There have been two tendencies over the centuries. The dominant one has been to denigrate the Quran at every opportunity, along with Muhammad. The attack on the Quran has followed several lines. First, its literary style has been targeted. Thomas Carlyle said: "It is a toilsome reading as I ever undertook, a wearisome, confused jumble, crude." Second, Christians have often regarded the Quran as ultimately a product of demonic inspiration given Muhammad's denial of Christ's deity and his death on the Cross.

In recent years there has been a more moderate attitude to the Quran among some Christian scholars. This can be explained on several grounds. The beauty of the Arabic language used in the Quran has offset frequent complaints about some of the English translations. Further, even in English, some sections of the Quran are powerful in their rhetoric and read like some of the Psalms in the Old Testament.

More important, scholars like Kenneth Cragg and Hans Küng have argued that the Quran brought much light and truth to pagan Arabia, even if it did not bring the full light of the gospel. Christians should rejoice at every truth advanced by the Quran, this newer view suggests. After all, would we prefer that Muhammad had retained his pagan religious heritage?

Given the lofty monotheism of the Quran, it is proper, Küng would suggest, to refer to it, in some sense, as a word from God. Küng is developing a line of argument suggested by Wilfred Cantwell Smith about forty years ago. Smith, one of the most famous Christian scholars of Islam, believed that a proper reaction to the divine truths in the Quran demanded recognition of its divine inspiration, at least in part.

In one sense we have inherited three different views of the Quran: (a) in orthodox Islam it is the perfect word of God, never to be questioned; (b) in traditional Christianity it is a boring book that is a product of Hell; and (c) in liberal Christianity it is a partial word from God. Let me suggest my own view, one that has been influenced by the last two perspectives.

I was raised in a conservative Christian

In recent years there has been a more moderate attitude to the Quran among some Christian scholars.

52

setting where it would never be entertained that any book except the Bible could be inspired by God. So, my background leads me to have initial sympathies for the traditional Christian viewpoint. However, while earning my

> Fundamentally, the Quran is not giving a Christian message.

Ph.D. degree I studied with Hans Küng on Islam and other religions, as mentioned earlier. It is hard not to be impressed by his immense learning, his passion for truth, and his patience as a teacher.

In one class Küng invited Wilfred Cantwell Smith to be a guest. I was one of four students given the opportunity to quiz Smith on his views of Islam. Even with my disagreements with Professor Smith, it was obvious how well he knew the Islamic world (through study and firsthand experience) and the Quran. I was also impressed by his warm and open attitude to our questions. Here was the founder of the Center for the Study of World Religions at Harvard, one of the greatest living Islamic scholars, and he treated the class with utter kindness and humility, even as we expressed concern about some of his views.

So, how do I balance my traditional Christian convictions with the powerful impact of views from Professor Küng and Smith? In the end, I think there is something dangerous and helpful in both perspectives. In the conservative assessment of the Quran, the danger lies in losing opportunity for mission and truth-telling by overstatement of the negative characteristics of the Quran. Of course, on the positive side, this negativity preserves a warning about anti-Christian teachings in the Quran. *Fundamentally, the Quran is not giving a Christian message.*

The danger in Küng and Smith is that they overstate the positive elements in the Quran. Consequently they give to Muhammad a prophetic mantle which is surely not consistent with his ignorance and denial of key elements of the Christian faith. Likewise, it is very problematic to give the Quran any divine status when its message is fundamentally directed toward Muhammad, not Jesus, and to Mecca, not Calvary.

This does not demand that we dismiss Küng and Smith total-ly. If they have overstated the merits of both Muhammad and the Quran, at least they have seen the real merits of both. They have resisted the impulse that runs deep in conservative Christianity to make the gospel look good by making other religions look worse than they really are, which amounts to bearing false witness. If we care about truth as followers of Jesus, our critique of the Quran must be truthful.

In the final analysis, any positive things Christians can say about the Quran must be thoroughly tempered by recognition of its major weaknesses. The Quran illustrates no pervasive knowledge of either the Old or New Testament, making it easy to argue that the Quran is a product of human authorship, not divine inspiration. This is especially true given the ways in which the Quran distorts the Gospel message of God's love in Jesus Christ, his eternal Son. We can now turn our full attention to the picture of Jesus presented in Islam.

REFLECTING ON LESSON FOUR

1. How do you think the Bible is different than the Quran?

2. What differences do you see between the Islamic and Christian views of God? How would you explain the Trinity to a Muslim?

3. What do *you* think should be the proper Christian attitude toward the Quran?

4. Can you understand why Küng and Smith argue that Christians should view the Quran as a partial word from God? What is your reaction to that?

5. Are you interested in reading the Quran? Should Christians read the Quran?

5
F I V E

JESUS AND ISLAM

The ultimate measure of Islam, from a Christian perspective, is to see what this religion has to say about Jesus of Nazareth. The previous chapters on Muhammad and the Quran hinted at key issues about Jesus. It is now time to make this an explicit focus of our study.

INITIAL OBSERVATIONS

Before we get into details, several preliminary points are important. We must remind ourselves again that Islam and other religions represent different universes of understanding. We often assume that people in other faiths look at the world the way we do. Of course, we share some things in common. But, the differences usually make all the difference in the world.

This is especially important about Jesus. Because Jesus is so central to Christians, we tend to think that he is a central figure in other religions as well. That is simply not true. We can be confused on this for several reasons. We are told frequently that all religions are basically the same. From this we could erroneously assume that Jesus is pre-eminent in other faiths, just as he is in Christian faith. Further, we can be unduly influenced by the truth that people in other religions speak highly of Jesus. Again, while Jesus is praised in almost all faiths, this does not mean that he is granted central focus and supreme worship.

When I take classes to visit leaders of other religions, it is often a real shock for students to realize that Jesus is not given significant attention in Hinduism, Buddhism, Judaism, and Islam. Students are perplexed and hurt by this absence. And, more than anything they are deeply saddened. What becomes clear to them is that Jesus hardly appears on the radar screen of other religions.

Just as Muhammad gets virtually no time in the reflections of North American Christians, most Muslims give little attention to the claims of Jesus Christ. Most Jews spend little time pondering the Gospels just as Christians devote few moments to contemplation of Talmudic law. Most Buddhists, especially those in the far east, think seldom about Jesus or even the existence of God. Orthodox Buddhism teaches that there is no God.

Christians must also face the fact that even when other religions express a positive outlook about Jesus, the understanding of Jesus is often different than the one offered in the New Testament. I remember once going to a psychic fair to study on the latest trends in the occult world. I had done a lot of study on the New Age movement at the time but was only beginning to seriously examine the history and teachings of witchcraft. I met a witch at one of the booths and in the course of conversation I asked her about Jesus. I was somewhat taken back when she replied that she believed in Jesus.

What this reflects is something negative and positive. Sadly, Jesus is often betrayed with a kiss, sometimes consciously (as in the case of Judas) but usually unintentionally (as in her case). I don't believe this witch knew that her wiccan beliefs were utterly inconsistent with her words of appreciation about Jesus. On the positive side, the affirmation of Jesus can lead to an opportunity for witness, however. The professed

Muhammad gets virtually no time in the reflections of Christians, and most Muslims give little attention to the claims of Jesus Christ.

56

admiration for Jesus can be used as a launching pad for inviting deeper consideration of the claims of Jesus.

A Muslim man was cleaning the carpets in our home one day. It was time for him to pray and he was outside in our driveway figuring out which way to face Mecca. I asked him if he wanted to pray inside for privacy. He declined but my openness to him led to a deeper conversation. When I mentioned the name of Jesus, he spoke with respect. This was a chance to share my understanding of the Gospel. Even though it was difficult to get beyond the barriers between our faiths, the name of Jesus was raised in common if not equal interest.

> Jesus is given a muted and distorted presence in the Quran, where He is named in just 28 of over 6,000 verses.

JESUS IN THE QURAN

When a Christian first hears from Christian scholars that the Quran can be a further word of God to the church, this would lean almost any believer to expect that Jesus commands a dominant presence in the Quran, just as he does in the New Testament. Sadly, this is far from the case, and it is one signal that the liberal Christian assessment of the Quran is far too optimistic.

As I did research for this study guide, I checked several indexes of the Quran as a way of monitoring the fairness of my emphases. One comprehensive index of the Quran was provided in a reference book, and I also did several searches on the Internet. There are hundreds of Muslim web sites, and so I examined them to assure the accuracy of my analysis of the Quranic material on Jesus. Sadly, the evidence is conclusive that *Jesus is given a muted and distorted presence in the Quran.*

There are over 6,000 verses in the Quran. Consider a word search in one of the famous translations of the Quran. *Jesus is named in just 28 of the verses in the entire Islamic scripture.* In stark contrast, the name of Jesus is on virtually every page of the New Testament. This is a strong signal that something is tragically amiss, and that there can be no harmony, in an ultimate sense, between the Gospel presentation of Jesus and the perspective given in the Quran.

When these 28 verses are examined, the situation becomes even more bleak. If this body of material reflected a view of Jesus consistent with the New Testament, then the scarcity of references would be understandable. However, what emerges from reading the Quranic material is the fact that Muhammad was never really introduced to the biblical portrait of the Lord Jesus Christ. Muhammad's self-assumed prophetic mantle and the weight of alleged Quranic revelation has led millions of Muslims into an impoverished vision of Jesus.

Of course, this needs some examination. Since this material on Jesus is absolutely crucial to understand the Islamic faith, all of the verses are given in the appendix. This is a way for you to see for yourself the Quranic teaching. Here we can ask about the overall meaning of these passages.

What is most striking about these twenty-eight verses is what little they offer about the ministry and identity of Jesus. Only six passages give substantial data! *If Muslims look only to the Quran for a picture of Jesus, there is little hope that they will learn the truth about the Savior.* Overall, there are ten significant teachings about Jesus in the whole material.

1. Allah has sent Jesus as an Apostle and Prophet and given him strength through the Holy Spirit. Jesus is the Word from God and is to be honored as a righteous man and as the bearer of a covenant with God. See Surahs 2:87; 2:253; 3:45; 19:34; and 33:7. Surah 3:45 reads: "Behold! the angels said: 'O Mary! God giveth thee glad tidings of a Word from Him: his name will be Christ Jesus, the son of Mary, held in honour in this world and the Hereafter and of (the company of) those nearest to God.'"

> If Muslims look only to the Quran for a picture of Jesus, there is little hope that they will learn the truth about the Savior.

2. Jesus received and **taught the same message** that was given to Muhammad.

This message was given earlier to Adam, Abraham, Noah, Moses, and other prophets. This is taught in Surahs 2:136; 3:3; 3:84; 4:163 and 42:13. Surah 3:84 reads: "Say: 'We believe in God, and in what has been revealed to us and what was revealed to Abraham, Isma'il [Ishmael], Isaac, Jacob, and the Tribes, and in (the Books) given to Moses, Jesus, and the prophets, from their Lord: We make no distinction between one and another among them, and to God do we bow our will (in Islam).'"

The Quran portrays Jesus as a model of virtue and wisdom.

3. The **disciples of Jesus were called Muslims** in New Testament times. Surah 3:52 states: "When Jesus found Unbelief on their part He said: 'Who will be My helpers to (the work of) God?' Said the disciples: 'We are God's helpers: We believe in God, and do thou bear witness that we are Muslims.'" This belief solidifies the Islamic view that theirs is the true religion. "After all," the Muslim can say, "the followers of the gospel were Muslims just like us!"

4. *Jesus is a model of virtue and wisdom.* This is taught in Surahs 43:57 and 43:63. The latter states: "When Jesus came with Clear Signs, he said: 'Now have I come to you with Wisdom, and in order to make clear to you some of the (points) on which ye dispute: therefore fear God and obey me.'"

5. Jesus did **not die on the cross at Calvary.** This most famous of Islamic teachings is mentioned in just one verse of the Quran, but this sole passage is backed up by the weight of Islamic tradition. Surah 4:157 settles the matter for the Muslim world. After talking about those who boasted: "We killed Christ Jesus, the son of Mary, the Apostle of God," it says "but they killed him not, nor crucified him, but so it was made to appear to them, and those who differ therein are full of doubts, with no (certain) knowledge, but only conjecture to follow, for of a surety they killed him not."

Muslims believe that God would never let Jesus die the death of a common criminal. This view is based on the argument that a true prophet's work is marked by ultimate success, as in the case of Muhammad. So, *Islamic tradition teaches that God allowed someone else to die in place of Jesus.* This is often held to be Judas or Simon (who carried the cross). There are a few Muslim scholars who affirm that Jesus died on the cross because of the weight of historical testimony to that fact. However, even they do not believe that Jesus died for the sins of the world.

6. Jesus was raised to heaven with Allah to vindicate the message of Jesus against his enemies. This is stated in Surah 3:55 "Behold! God said: 'O Jesus! I will take thee and raise thee to Myself and clear thee (of the falsehoods) of those who blaspheme; I will make those who follow thee superior to those who reject faith, to the Day of Resurrection: Then shall ye all return unto me, and I will judge between you of the matters wherein ye dispute.'" This is **not** a reference to the resurrection of Jesus at Easter. Muslims deny that Christian doctrine. This verse is, rather, the basis for Islamic belief that Jesus was preserved from death and taken directly to heaven.

7. According to the Quran, Jesus is not the son of God and the Trinity doctrine is untrue. Surah 4:171 is explicit on this: "People of the Book! Commit no excesses in your religion: Nor say of God aught but the truth. Christ Jesus the son of Mary was (no more than) an apostle of God, and His Word, which He bestowed on Mary, and a spirit proceeding from Him: so believe in God and His apostles. Say not 'Trinity.' Desist: it will be better for you: for God is one God: Glory be to Him: (far exalted is He) above having a son."

The Islamic denial of the deity of Christ and the Trinity is also taught in Surah 5:119, a passage which also illustrates Muslim misunderstanding of what Christians believe by the Trinity. The verse reads: "And behold! God will say: 'O Jesus the son of Mary! Didst thou say unto men, worship me and my mother as gods in derogation of God?' He will say: 'Glory to Thee! never could I say what I had no right (to say).'"

Islamic tradition teaches that God allowed someone else to die in place of Jesus.

8. The Quran teaches that Jesus performed many miracles. The most explicit statement about the miraculous

60

work of Jesus is given in Surah 5:113. It reads: "Then will God say: 'O Jesus the son of Mary! Recount My favour to thee and to thy mother. . . . Behold! thou makest out of clay, as it were, the figure of a bird, by My leave, and thou

The Quran affirms the Virgin Birth of Jesus.

breathest into it and it becometh a bird by My leave, and thou healest those born blind, and the lepers, by My leave. And behold! thou bringest forth the dead by My leave. And behold! I did restrain the Children of Israel from (violence to) thee when thou didst show them the clear Signs, and the unbelievers among them said: "This is nothing but evident magic."'"

Obviously, Christians should celebrate the agreement with Scripture on the miracles of Jesus. However, things are not completely in order. This story of the clay bird taking flight is from later Christian lore, not the authentic Gospel material. Despite this, the miraculous work of Jesus provides an open door for Muslim exploration of the biblical stories about Jesus, where his works led to recognition that he was the Son of God.

9. *The Quran affirms the Virgin Birth of Jesus.* This is clear from the dialogue between Mary and an angel recorded in Surah 19:20-21, a conversation that parallels the Gospel accounts. Problems arise from the fact that the Quran records that the birth of Jesus took place under a palm tree. As well, when Mary brought the infant to her relatives, they said: "How can we talk to one who is in the cradle?" The reply came from Jesus himself: "Lo! I am the slave of Allah. He hath given me the Scripture and hath appointed me a prophet" (Surah 19:30).

10. The Quran teaches that **Jesus predicted the ministry of Muhammad**. This is a famous Islamic view. The relevant Quranic passage reads: "And remember, Jesus, the son of Mary, said: 'O Children of Israel! I am the apostle of God (sent) to you, confirming the Law (which came) before me, and giving Glad Tidings of an Apostle to come after me, whose name shall be Ahmad'" (61:6). Muslims contend that

the Paraclete mentioned by Jesus in the Gospel of John is **not** the Holy Spirit; it is the prediction of the coming of Muhammad.

What is one to make of this? First, it is inconsistent for Muslims to pick out a few verses of the Bible to support their views when the whole weight of Scripture is against them. If they trust the Bible about the coming of Muhammad, how can they avoid its undeniable message that Jesus is the Son of God, God in the flesh, and that he died on the cross? As well, the Bible is clear that Jesus is the Savior and Lord.

Second, on the specific teaching in John, the message is obvious to everyone except Muslims. Jesus is talking about the ministry of the Holy Spirit. The three chapters in John that focus on the Spirit (14-16) are abundantly clear. Muslims engage in exegetical sleight of hand to try to deny the obvious. The Comforter to come is the Spirit, not Muhammad. The passages in Acts that talk about the promise and arrival of the Spirit further confirm traditional Christian convictions.

CONCLUDING ANALYSIS

Christians must strongly deny five of the ten key Quranic teachings on Jesus. These are noted in bold print below. Does this mean we agree with the other five? Not at all. We could affirm a "Christian" understanding of some of the remaining ideas but cannot accept them from an Islamic perspective. On the items marked with an asterisk, there is a serious disagreement between the Christian and Muslim meaning of the words.

For example, both religions affirm Jesus as prophet and apostle, but in Christianity he is greater than both realities. Likewise, both groups teach that Jesus ascended to heaven. In the Bible Jesus ascends to heaven after his postresurrection appearances to the disciples. In Islam, there is no Calvary and no Easter. Jesus ascends to heaven sometime after he avoided the crucifixion.

Christians must strongly deny five of the ten key Quranic teachings on Jesus.

1. *Allah has sent Jesus as an Apostle and Prophet.

2. **Jesus received and taught the same message that was given to Muhammad.**

> **The Gospels are foreign documents to the Muslim world.**

3. **The disciples of Jesus were called Muslims in New Testament times.**

4. Jesus is a model of virtue and wisdom.

5. **Jesus did not die on the cross at Calvary.**

6. *Jesus was raised to heaven with Allah to vindicate the message of Jesus.

7. **Jesus is not the son of God and the Trinity doctrine is untrue.**

8. Jesus performed many miracles.

9. The Quran affirms the Virgin Birth of Jesus.

10. **Jesus predicted the ministry of Muhammad.**

Our discussion shows that the Quran teaching on Jesus is very inadequate. It offers a very distorted picture of the Savior in what it affirms. Further, the Quran's utter failure about Jesus is shown by what it neglects. There is virtually no teaching from Jesus in the Quran. *The Gospels are foreign documents to the Muslim world.* Likewise, the Quran knows nothing of the teaching of the rest of the New Testament, including the absolutely crucial data from the apostle Paul.

Since Muslims believe the Bible has been corrupted by Jews and Christians, they do not turn to it as a source of authority. Consequently, the Gospel accounts are not checked in order to verify the accuracy of the Quran about Jesus. In the end, a presupposition rules the day. The Quran is the proper guide to Jesus and everything else, according to Islam. Therefore, the evidence of the New Testament does not matter. This leads to Muslim ignorance and denial of the true identity and work of Jesus Christ. Nothing could represent a greater loss for a world religion that claims one in six of every people on our planet.

REFLECTING ON LESSON FIVE

1. How would you approach a Muslim on the question of Jesus' death on the cross?

2. How would you use the Muslim belief in Jesus' miracles and virgin birth as starting points from which to witness to them?

3. List the five points on which Muslims and Christians strongly disagree.

4. List the two points on which Muslims and Christians agree with reservations.

5. List the three points on which Muslims and Christians agree. How are these three points still problematic?

6. How would you explain Muhammad's overall understanding of Jesus? What does it suggest about his awareness of the New Testament?

6

S I X

THE CHRISTIAN WITNESS TO ISLAM

In previous chapters we explored the proper study of Islam, its basics, the prophet Muhammad, the Quran, and the place of Jesus in Islam. Given what we know, we can move on to concrete proposals for an effective witness to Muslims. How do we "speak the truth in love" to those who follow Allah? How do we point to Jesus to those who are so radically devoted to Muhammad? What can help us to share the Bible's teaching to those who believe it has been replaced by the Quran?

TEN COMMANDMENTS FOR TRUTH TELLERS

Over the years I have done my share of witnessing with people in other religions. I will talk at length with Mormons and Jehovah's Witnesses who come to my door. I visit the leaders of other religions, read their publications, and seek to be an effective witness for Jesus Christ. In hundreds of conversations with people of other faiths, including Muslims, I have learned, both through success and failure, some very important truths in telling the truth. So, here are ten commandments for truth tellers.

Commandment One: *Remember that the battle is the Lord's.* Nothing hurts Christian witness like our belief that everything depends on you and me. This command is not to deny our responsibility, but, rather, to put our responsibility in its proper place. God is sovereign and Jesus is Lord even in the face of the threat represented by Islam, even with the daunting task of trying to help Muslims see the beauty of Jesus.

My twin brother Bob was listening to my long list of "things to do" one day. He sensed my anxiety and pressure. He asked me quite casually: "Do you have nail prints on your hands?" I quickly answered no, before thinking what he was getting at. When I replied he said: "Well, you're not the Savior of the world, are you?" As we think about witness to Muslims, let's remember who the Savior is, and this will give us peace for the task.

Commandment Two: *Remember that Love is the most important weapon in Christian witness.* The previous chapters have focused a lot on intellectual, theological and biblical material. You have "learned" foundational material that can help you for the rest of your life. However, the emphasis on intellectual learning about Islam, as important as it is, will amount to nothing if your witness to Muslims is not rooted in love.

In fact, evidence from missionaries to Islam suggests that loving presence is the most important ingredient in Christian proclamation. I am not scared of debate or intellectual arguments, but by this I do not mean red-faced, foaming at the mouth. But, even with my openness to the right kind of debate, I want you to remember that loving action is the most important witness to the Muslims you meet.

Commandment Three: *Lose battles to win wars.* While this does not sound like a very loving principle (battles? wars?), it is simply employing a military metaphor to suggest the importance of priorities. Consider a fact mentioned earlier in this guide. According to Muslim tradition, part of the proof for Muhammad's prophetic status lies in the fact that he had special physical signs on his back. We might refer to them as "moles."

> Remember that Love is the most important weapon in Christian witness.

What do you do with this fact? Robert Morey writes a pamphlet called "By their Moles you shall know them" and makes this a focus for evangelism. Morey is not impressed by a mole on someone's back. While I have much respect for almost everything that Morey writes, I really think that it would be better to give up this particular battle for the sake of a larger strategy.

> Some Muslims will be helped through debate. Others will be won over by reading the Gospel stories.

I suggest this for two reasons. First, we can no longer prove absolutely what were the actual physical marks on Muhammad's body. Second, and more important, I think most Muslims would find this kind of attack too direct. It has an "in your face" quality to it that could hurt overall witness on much more important things.

Commandment Four: *Different Strokes for Different Folks.* You should be very skeptical of anyone who tells you: "there is just one way to witness to Muslims." God is a God of variety, and he knows that individuals are reached in radically different methods. *Some Muslims will be helped through debate. Others will be won over by reading the Gospel stories* about Jesus. Many Muslims are touched by the loving help of Christians who have become their friends. A few might even be won by reference to the "mole" question!

When you meet a Muslim neighbor, for example, do your best to assess the particular situation of this Muslim. What is their background? How devoted are they to Islam? Do they seem to be the type who can handle disagreements? Do they really care about truth? Can you help them in some way?

Commandment Five: *Don't Think You are the Lone Ranger!* James Ryle, one of the leaders in Promise Keepers, showed up one time to preach in his church in Boulder and he was dressed like the Lone Ranger. That made an interesting start to his sermon. He had the attention of everyone. What he did next was very important. He took off his mask and said: "The days of the Lone Ranger are over!"

You and I are not alone in the witness to the Muslim world. In fact, like the author of Hebrews states, we are surrounded by a great cloud of witnesses. We are joined by thousands of missionaries who have given up home and security to reach the Muslim world. We are joined by martyrs who have shed their blood, willing to pay the ultimate price for daring to follow Jesus in mission.

We are also joined by scholars who have spent years to understand Islam in an accurate way. Some of the best scholars are not Christians but they care deeply about true and accurate information. We learn from them. Likewise, there are many mission organizations that focus on reaching Muslims for Jesus. We are not alone.

Commandment Six: *Remember the power of belief systems to blind people.* It would be convenient if this command was simply about non-Christians who are blind to reality. However, Christians can be blind to things because of our belief system. This is not saying anything against the gospel or biblical teaching. Rather, mixed in with true gospel teaching are prejudices and dogmatic opinions that are not true. So, we must ask the Spirit to open our eyes to see if and when we are wrong on particular items.

This applies, of course, to the power of the Islamic belief system to blind Muslims to the truth of the gospel. It helps for us as we witness to look at things through the eyes of the Muslim. Consider how the gospel looks to him or her. Think what it is like to have never heard the truth about Jesus but only to have heard since childhood that Christians do not love Muhammad! In fact, *Muslims believe we hate Muhammad so much that we deliberately changed our Bible* so that it no longer gives the same message as the Quran.

Commandment Seven: *Remember that the battle is spiritual.* The mission to the Islamic world involves a battle far more important than one that is intellectual, cultural, or political. Whether Muslims represent a real political threat to the United States is an important question to ask. However, the battle for the souls of Muslims is a far more important issue, and that

> Muslims believe we hate Muhammad so much that we deliberately changed our Bible.

68

involves an incredible spiritual battle. Once we really believe this, it will do something to our prayer life, and to the passion that we bring to our witness.

Paul tells us in 2 Corinthians 4 that the weapons of our warfare are not carnal. In other words, we are not interested in bombs or guns. Rather, our weapons are spiritual and they must be since it is a spiritual battle given, as Paul states, that Satan has blinded the minds of unbelievers lest they come to the light of the gospel.

> The religions of the world have many things in common; the crucial difference is the person of Jesus Christ.

Commandment Eight: *Ask for the guidance of the Holy Spirit.* Given that the mission of the Church is spiritual, what can be more important than asking for the aid of the Comforter in witnessing. Pray and ask God to lead you as you talk to Muslims. Ask the Holy Spirit to give you the right words, to show you the right path, and to guide you as you seek to witness in word and/or deed.

In research for this book I have heard wonderful accounts of the work of the Spirit to open the eyes of Muslims. These have sometimes involved stories of healings, in one case involving a very prominent Muslim leader from Egypt who gave his life to Jesus. One of my students who has a special burden for Muslims told me recently of cases where God used dreams and visions to show Muslims their need to accept Jesus as their Savior and Lord.

Commandment Nine: *Focus on Jesus.* Twenty years ago I had the privilege to meet Stephen Neill, the famous Anglican writer, teacher, and missionary. Neill, a very quiet and gentle man, knew the realities of Christian witness to other religions firsthand. He said one thing at the time that I have never forgotten. He pointed out in a chapel address that *the religions of the world have many things in common.* He said *the crucial difference is the person of Jesus Christ.*

There is nothing more important than to focus on Jesus as we share with Muslims. This makes everything else we do pale in contrast. To point to Jesus is the greatest act of witness we can make. I regret the times that I have lost ground in witness because I have spent too much time in debate or argument. Or, I have pushed some new bit of evidence that shows the weakness of the other religion. This stuff has its place, but it *must remain in the background to an intense preoccupation with witness about the King of Kings and Lord of Lords.*

Commandment Ten: *Know When to Stop.* Jesus was much more realistic about the human condition than many of his followers. He knew the hearts of humans and he recognized that some people do not want to hear the gospel. This is why he told his followers that there is a time to stop witnessing and move on to others.

There is no way to be certain when we have reached that point. Further, it is better to err on the side of mercy and patience than to prematurely halt our witness to given individuals. However, there is a time to stop, and it could hurt Christian witness by continued talking. We must also remember that God can bring others later to build on the witness that we have left.

CRUCIAL QUESTIONS IN MUSLIM DIALOGUE

We can now focus on some particular issues that always arise in the Christian dialogue with Muslims. To handle these, let me put them in the form of a question and then give some helpful answers.

Question: How do I defend the Trinity when Muslims say that this contradicts Christian belief in one God?

My advice here is first to admit that the Trinity doctrine is very difficult to understand. However, that something is difficult to comprehend is no proof that it is untrue, otherwise we would not believe that God is everywhere (how can he do that?) or that the space shuttle can fly so fast. The main point to make on the Trinity is that it is the

> Arguments against other religions must remain in the background to an intense preoccupation with witness about the King of Kings and Lord of Lords.

70

witness of God in the New Testament, and it is based on the very teaching of Jesus Christ.

Question: How do I defend the New Testament when Muslims say that there are different versions of Greek manuscripts?

The textual transmission or copying of the New Testament is proof of its authenticity.

Basically, the Muslim is playing trivial pursuit here. The differences between what is said in one manuscript versus another involve minor differences that do not have any impact on the basic teaching of the New Testament. Actually, *the textual transmission or copying of the New Testament is proof of its authenticity* and also proof that the Muslim view of the gospels is rooted in blind obedience to the Quran's teaching.

You might also say to the Muslim that there is something contradictory in a prophet who points to previous scripture as proof of his message but shows little awareness of the vast body of material in this scripture. Muslims, of course, show little interest in serious historical investigation of the Bible, and they are far from open to the possibility that Muhammad may have deceived them by his own limited and distorted knowledge of Jesus.

Question: What do I say to the Muslim who argues that the Quran is the greatest miracle performed by Allah?

I would recommend three strategies here. First, rather than disagree, you might use the Quran to point to Jesus. Ask the Muslim if she would be willing to study about Jesus since he was so influential in God's witness before Muhammad. Second, you could dispute the Muslim claim by engaging in a debate about the Quran's integrity and greatness. You need to make sure you know what you are talking about before you take this second approach. If you have not read the Quran, your point will sound rather weak. Third, you might want to challenge the Muslim to read the Gospel of John and ask him what part of the Quran he would like you to read.

Question: What if the Muslim says that Christians are bigoted against Arabs and they are always supporting Israel?

On first impulse, you should admit that *western Christians often portray Arabs in a bigoted way*. For this we should apologize. We forget that not all Arabs are Muslim; what about our Arab Christian brothers and sisters? (Of course, even if all Arabs were Muslims this would not justify any bigotry or prejudice on our part.) Second, you can also admit that our tendency to support Israel has sometimes blinded us to mistreatment of Muslims by Israel.

Third, for the sake of balance, you might note the pervasive Islamic hatred of Israel, and ask if this is consistent with the Quran's command for Muslims to allow both Jews and Christians freedom to practice their own religion. Finally, it might simply be better to move quickly beyond these political questions to issues of Christian witness about Jesus.

Question: What if the Muslim complains that Christian women are immodest and do not wear veils?

You should point out that one must not confuse the practices of western society as equal to what Christians believe. You might admit that some standards of dress are immodest according to Muslim standards but that cultural factors do play some part in deciding what is right and wrong on secondary items. You could also ask about the lack of freedom afforded to Muslim women in many Arab countries.

The issue of women's rights is obviously central in our day. There is strong debate over what part culture plays in making ultimate decisions. Many Muslim women say that they love wearing some sort of veil. Is this not their right? Must all women be unveiled to prove they are free? A Christian witness here would probably hope for the kind of lengthy contact to see what is actually going on in a given context. Are the relevant women really free?

Question: What should I say if a Muslim asks me about the source for Muhammad's teaching? Do I say it is from Satan?

Western Christians often portray Arabs in a bigoted way.

I think the right answer is to say something like this: "While I do not believe Muhammad received his revelations

72

from God, I believe that he was a sincere person and that he taught some crucial truths that the Arab people needed to hear. Most certainly, he was not a Satanist. Since I do not believe he even knew the full revelation of God in Jesus, I think he was confused on his calling as a prophet."

> It is better to avoid direct attack, and engage in a more subtle analysis.

You might think my answer lacks courage. No, it is not that. It is more about remembering the earlier principle: lose a battle to win a war. It is counterproductive to tell Muslims that Muhammad is from Satan, or that he heard Satan's voice instead of the angel Gabriel. *I think it is better to avoid this direct attack, and engage in a more subtle analysis.* In the end, I believe that Muhammad's revelations are a product of his own dysfunctional background, the confusing things he heard about the Bible from others, and his own desires to be a religious leader.

Question: What if a Muslim asks me something about Islam and I have no idea what she is talking about?

There is no need to panic. No one can know everything about Islam. Why not ask the Muslim to clarify her question and ask for help from her in getting to know Islam better? One of the things I had to overcome in writing this book is the feeling that I have not covered everything. My feeling here is simply absurd, on one level. How can an introductory study guide tell you everything? I have tried to be content with writing a study guide that is accurate and fair in everything that it says.

On this latter point, one thing for you (and your group) to remember is that Muslims come from different backgrounds and groups, just like Christians. For the most part, you are most likely to meet a Sunni Muslim. Virtually nine out of ten Muslims follow the Sunni version of Islam. They differ with the smaller but more famous branch of Islam known as Shi'ite. The latter have received enormous attention because of their dominance in Iran. The differences between Sunni and Shi'ite Islam revolve chiefly around the way they view succession of leadership after Muhammad.

Of course, there are other types of Muslims. Sufi Muslims emphasize a mystical interpretation of Islam. There are also minor Islamic groups in the Middle East and other countries. In America, there are some radical groups like the Nation of Islam that get more attention from the media than the more dominant traditions like Sunni.

Question: What if the Muslim asks me to share just one reason why he should leave the great faith of Islam?

The answer is simple. Muslims should leave Islam in order to embrace Jesus, the Savior and Lord. Jesus said one time that it is worth it to give up everything in order to gain the pearl of great price. That pearl is the gospel, and the gospel is Jesus. The Muslim gains a Savior who is above the Law since he is Lord of the Law. This solves the issue of legalism. The Muslim gains a friend since Jesus died for him. This solves the issue of lack of assurance in Islam. The Muslim gains peace over sin and death since he gains "the Prince of Peace" who conquered both through Calvary and the Empty Tomb.

Question: What if I am asked if we worship the same God as Muslims?

I would recommend three different emphases here. First, make it clear that we share some common views about the one God who created heaven and earth. For example, we agree with Muslim belief in only one God and that he is omnipotent, omniscient, and omnipresent. Second, we must also explain where we have totally different views of God. We believe that God's full revelation is given in his eternal Son Jesus. Muslims do not share this vision at all. Further, the revelation in Jesus illustrates a different view of God's love and grace. It is very instructive that the Quran does not even once assert that "God is love." Third, we should present the warnings of Jesus (whom Muslims recognize as a true prophet) against those who fail to follow him as the one Son of the one eternal God.

REFLECTING ON LESSON SIX

1. Can you remember a situation where you have given ground on a point in order to be in a better position to win someone to the gospel?

2. Do you know anyone who is specifically reaching out to Muslims either in the United States or overseas? What have been their experiences?

3. What would your response be to the charge that American women are immodest?

4. How would you respond if a Muslim asked you where you believe Muhammad got his revelations?

5. Do Christians and Muslims worship the same God?

6. Have you ever hurt your witness by losing your temper in debate with a Muslim?

7. How can your church show love to Muslims?

APPENDIX: JESUS IN THE QURAN

1. Surah 2:87

We gave Moses the Book and followed him up with a succession of apostles; We gave Jesus the son of Mary Clear (Signs) and strengthened him with the holy spirit. Is it that whenever there comes to you an apostle with what ye yourselves desire not, ye are puffed up with pride? Some ye called impostors, and others ye slay!

2. Surah 2:136

Say ye: "We believe in God, and the revelation given to us, and to Abraham, Isma'il, Isaac, Jacob, and the Tribes, and that given to Moses and Jesus, and that given to (all) prophets from their Lord: We make no difference between one and another of them: And we bow to God (in Islam)."

3. Surah 2:253

Those apostles We endowed with gifts, some above others: To one of them God spoke; others He raised to degrees (of honour); to Jesus the son of Mary We gave clear (Signs), and strengthened him with the holy spirit. If God had so willed, succeeding generations would not have fought among each other, after clear (Signs) had come to them, but they (chose) to wrangle, some believing and others rejecting. If God had so willed, they would not have fought each other; but God fulfilleth His plan.

4. Surah 3:3

It is He Who sent down to thee (step by step), in truth, the Book, confirming what went before it; and He sent down the Law (of Moses) and the Gospel (of Jesus) before this, as a guide to mankind, and He sent down the criterion (of judgment between right and wrong).

5. Surah 3:45

Behold! the angels said: "O Mary! God giveth thee glad tidings of a Word from Him: his name will be Christ Jesus, the son of Mary, held in honour in this world and the Hereafter and of (the company of) those nearest to God.

6. Surah 3:52

When Jesus found Unbelief on their part He said: "Who will be My helpers to (the work of) God?" Said the disciples: "We are God's helpers: We believe in God, and do thou bear witness that we are Muslims."

7. Surah 3:55

Behold! God said: "O Jesus! I will take thee and raise thee to Myself and clear thee (of the falsehoods) of those who blaspheme; I will make those who follow thee superior to those who reject faith, to the Day of Resurrection: Then shall ye all return unto me, and I will judge between you of the matters wherein ye dispute."

8. Surah 3:59

The similitude of Jesus before God is as that of Adam; He created him from dust, then said to him: "Be." And he was.

9. Surah 3:84

Say: "We believe in God, and in what has been revealed to us and what was revealed to Abraham, Isma'il, Isaac, Jacob, and the Tribes, and in (the Books) given to Moses, Jesus, and the prophets, from their Lord: We make no distinction between one and another among them, and to God do we bow our will (in Islam)."

10. Surah 4:157

That they said (in boast), "We killed Christ Jesus the son of Mary, the Apostle of God"; but they killed him not, nor crucified him, but so it was made to appear to them, and those who differ therein are full of doubts, with no (certain) knowledge, but only conjecture to follow, for of a surety they killed him not.

11. Surah 4:163

We have sent thee inspiration, as We sent it to Noah and the Messengers after him: we sent inspiration to Abraham, Isma'il, Isaac, Jacob and the Tribes, to Jesus, Job, Jonah, Aaron, and Solomon, and to David We gave the Psalms.

12. Surah 4:171

People of the Book! Commit no excesses in your religion: Nor say of God aught but the truth. Christ Jesus the son of Mary was (no more than) an apostle of God, and His Word, which He bestowed on Mary, and a spirit proceeding from Him: so believe in God and His apostles. Say not "Trinity": desist: it will be better for you: for God is one God: Glory be to Him: (far exalted is He) above having a son. To Him belong all things in the heavens and on earth. And enough is God as a Disposer of affairs.

13. Surah 5:49

And in their footsteps We sent Jesus the son of Mary, confirming the Law that had come before him: We sent him the Gospel: therein was guidance and light, and confirmation of the Law that had come before him: a guidance and an admonition to those who fear God.

14. Surah 5:81

Curses were pronounced on those among the Children of Israel who rejected Faith, by the tongue of David and of Jesus the son of Mary: because they disobeyed and persisted in excesses.

15. Surah 5:113

Then will God say: "O Jesus the son of Mary! Recount My favour to thee and to thy mother. Behold! I strengthened thee with the holy spirit, so that thou didst speak to the people in childhood and in maturity. Behold! I taught thee the Book and Wisdom, the Law and the Gospel and behold! thou makest out of clay, as it were, the figure of a bird, by My leave, and thou breathest into it and it becometh a bird by My leave, and thou healest those born blind, and the lepers, by My leave. And behold! thou bringest forth the dead by My leave. And behold! I did restrain the Children of Israel from (violence to) thee when thou didst show them the clear Signs, and the unbelievers among them said: 'This is nothing but evident magic.'"

16. Surah 5:115

Behold! the disciples, said: "O Jesus the son of Mary! can thy Lord send down to us a table set (with viands) from heaven?" Said Jesus: "Fear God, if ye have faith."

17. Surah 5:117

Said Jesus the son of Mary: "O God our Lord! Send us from heaven a table set (with viands), that there may be for us — for the first and the last of us — a solemn festival and a sign from thee; and provide for our sustenance, for thou art the best Sustainer (of our needs)."

18. Surah 5:119

And behold! God will say: "O Jesus the son of Mary! Didst thou say unto men, worship me and my mother as gods in derogation of God'?" He will say: "Glory to Thee! never could I say what I had no right (to say). Had I said such a thing, thou wouldst indeed have known it. Thou knowest what is in my heart, Thou I know not what is in Thine. For Thou knowest in full all that is hidden."

19. Surah 6:85

And Zakariya and John, and Jesus and Elias: all in the ranks of the righteous:

20. Surah 19:32-35

"(He) hath made me kind to my mother, and not overbearing or miserable;

"So peace is on me the day I was born, the day that I die, and the day that I shall be raised up to life (again)!"

Such (was) Jesus the son of Mary: (it is) a statement of truth, about which they (vainly) dispute.

It is not befitting to (the majesty of) God that He should beget a son.

21. Surah 33:7

And remember We took from the prophets their covenant: As (We did) from thee: from Noah, Abraham, Moses, and Jesus the son of Mary: We took from them a solemn covenant:

22. Surah 42:13

The same religion has He established for you as that which He enjoined on Noah — the which We have sent by inspiration to thee — and that which We enjoined on Abraham, Moses, and Jesus: Namely, that ye should remain steadfast in religion, and make no divisions therein: to those who worship other things than God, hard is the (way) to which thou callest them. God chooses to Himself those whom He pleases, and guides to Himself those who turn (to Him).

23. Surah 43:57

When (Jesus) the son of Mary is held up as an example, behold, thy people raise a clamour thereat (in ridicule)!

24. Surah 43:61

And (Jesus) shall be a Sign (for the coming of) the Hour (of Judgment): therefore have no doubt about the (Hour), but follow ye Me: this is a Straight Way.

25. Surah 43:63

When Jesus came with Clear Signs, he said: "Now have I come to you with Wisdom, and in order to make clear to you some of the (points) on which ye dispute: therefore fear God and obey me.

26. Surah 57:27

Then, in their wake, We followed them up with (others of) Our apostles: We sent after them Jesus the son of Mary, and bestowed on him the Gospel; and We ordained in the hearts of those who followed him Compassion and Mercy. But the Monasticism which they invented for themselves, We did not prescribe for them: (We commanded) only the seeking for the Good Pleasure of God; but that they did not foster as they should have done. Yet We bestowed, on those among them who believed, their (due) reward, but many of them are rebellious transgressors.

27. Surah 61:6

And remember, Jesus, the son of Mary, said: "O Children of Israel! I am the apostle of God (sent) to you, confirming the Law (which came) before me, and giving Glad Tidings of an Apostle to come after me, whose name shall be Ahmad." But when he came to them with Clear Signs, they said, "this is evident sorcery!"

28. Surah 61:14

O ye who believe! Be ye helpers of God: As said Jesus the son of Mary to the Disciples, "Who will be my helpers to (the work of) God?" Said the disciples, "We are God's helpers!" then a portion of the Children of Israel believed, and a portion disbelieved: But We gave power to those who believed, against their enemies, and they became the ones that prevailed.

CONCLUSION

As a teacher I often wonder about the impact of my teaching. The same goes for writing. Will this study guide really make a difference? My hope is that you and your group will pick up the implicit challenge of this book and use what you have learned to be an effective witness about Islam and to Muslims. Though I don't get to meet most of the people who read my books and articles, I count it a privilege to share with you from my years of study of Christian faith as it relates to world religions and Islam in particular.

When I studied with Hans Küng, the famous German theologian, during my doctoral work, I was amazed by the way he ended the course. He asked that whatever he had taught us that was false or misleading to let him take back to Germany to fix up. We could keep the rest that was true and helpful. Well, I feel the same way about this book. It covers a lot of issues, some very complex ones, and perhaps I did not say something in the right way, or perhaps I was not balanced or fair. Let me keep on working on these things. The rest that has been rewarding to you, please share with others.

On the bottom line, I trust that your study about Islam has been much more than just study. I hope that your understanding of the greatness of God's full revelation in Jesus

Christ has been deepened, and that your faith in Jesus has been enriched. This will provide a solid base for your interaction with Muslims and with others about the supremacy of Jesus over all things, including the mosque, the claims of Muhammad, and the teachings of the Quran.

RESOURCES

For full length book study, the best evangelical response to Islam can be found in Norman Geisler and Abdul Saleeb, *Answering Islam* (Grand Rapids: Baker, 1993). George Braswell, *Islam* (Nashville: Broadman and Holman, 1996) is a great overview about Islamic history, social customs, and beliefs. As well, pay close attention to the work of Dudley Woodberry, a professor at Fuller Seminary who has served as a missionary in Muslim countries. He is the editor of *Muslims and Christians on the Emmaus Road* (Monrovia: MARC, 1989). I also recommend *Ministry in Islamic Contexts* (Norway: Lausanne Committee for World Evangelization, 1996).

There are several Christian authors who have devoted their entire academic life to the study of Islam. Chief among them are Kenneth Cragg and William Montgomery Watt. Cragg is the author of *The Call of the Minaret* (Maryknoll: Orbis, 1989), and *Muhammad and the Christian* (Maryknoll: Orbis, 1984). Watt's works include a standard biography of Muhammad and a recent book on *Muslim-Christian Encounters* (London: Routledge, 1991). Hans Küng's treatment of Islam displays both his intellectual rigor and courage. See his *Christianity and the World Religions* (Garden City: Doubleday, 1986). While I think all three writers overestimate the prophetic status of Muhammad, their erudition on Islam is obvious.

Paul Marshall's new book *Their Blood Cries Out* (Dallas: Word, 1996) documents the persecution of Christians around the world, and gives details of the Muslim maltreatment of believers. Judith Miller's reporting on militant Islam is incredible. See her book *God has Ninety-Nine Names* (New York: Simon & Schuster, 1996). V.S. Naipaul's book *Among the Believers: An Islamic Journey* (New York: Penguin, 1982) is a rich social commentary.

For Muslim self-understanding I recommend that you read the works of scholars like Seyyed Nasr, who is a devout Sufi Muslim, and Fazlur Rahman, who taught at the University of Chicago. On the Quran you can check various famous translations by Mohammed Marmaduke Pickthall (*The Meaning of the Glorious Koran*) or Yusaf Ali (*Holy Qur'an*) or Arberry's *The Koran Interpreted.*

For organizations that have helpful material on Islam, write to:

International Institute for the Study of Islam and Christianity

St. Andrews Ct., St. Andrews Road, Plaistow,

London E13 8QD, United Kingdom

SIM

Box 7900, Charlotte, NC 28241-7900

CRI International

P.O. Box 7000, Rancho Santa Margarita, CA 92688-7000

The John Ankerberg Show

Box 8977, Chattanooga, TN 37411

ABOUT THE AUTHOR

James A. Beverley is a Professor of Theology and Ethics and Chair of the Theology Department at Tyndale Seminary in Toronto, Canada. Professor Beverley has specialized for over twenty years in the relationship of Christian faith to new and world religions. He has an Honors B.A. in Philosophy and the Master of Divinity Degree from Acadia University, the Masters in Theology from the University of Toronto, and did his Ph.D. at the Toronto School of Theology.

Dr. Beverley is an ordained minister in the Canadian Baptist Federation. He is a member of the Evangelical Theological Society, the American Academy of Religion, and other academic bodies. He has authored three previous books, and has written numerous essays for edited volumes, journals, and magazines. He is a frequent consultant to the media, and has been an expert witness in legal cases.

Readers who wish to interact with the author on the material in this book or who want to share their views and personal experiences can write to: Dr. James A. Beverley, Professor of Theology and Ethics, Tyndale Seminary, 25 Ballyconnor Court, Toronto, Ontario M2M 4B3 or e-mail at jbeverley@tyndale.ca.